BEAT THING

BEAT THING

DAVID MELTZER

La Alameda Press ∞ Albuquerque

Sections from this work appeared in *Shiny #9/10* (edited by Larry Fagin);
New American Writing #?? (edited by Paul Hoover and Maxine Chernoff);
"Beat Thing: Commentary" first appeared as a Big Bridge chapbook
(edited by Michael Rothenberg, illustrated by Nancy Victoria Davis).

Cover: Robert Briggs reading to jazz, The Cellar, 1959.
On the left is Leo Wright, alto saxophone; Bill Weisjahn, piano;
Max Hartstein, co-owner, bass; Sonny (last name?), co-owner, drums.
Photograph by C.R. Snyder
Copyright © 2003 by C.R. Snyder

Titlepage: David Meltzer reading in the "6" Gallery, 1958
Photograph by C.R. Snyder
Copyright © 2003 by C.R. Snyder

Back cover photograph:
"Wallace Berman, Peyote Eyes, Larkspur, 1960"
Photograph by Patricia Jordan
Archives of American Art, Smithsonian Institution.

ISBN: 1-888809-43-4

Library of Congress Cataloging-in-Publication Data

Meltzer, David.
  Beat thing / David Meltzer.
    p. cm.
  ISBN 1-888809-43-4 (alk. paper)
  1. Beat generation--Poetry. I. Title.
PS3563.E45B43 2004
811'.54--dc22

                          2004000981

La Alameda Press
9636 Guadalupe Trail NW
Albuquerque, New Mexico 87114

Max Hartstein at the ticket desk, The Cellar, 1959.
Photograph by C.R. Snyder

THE BEAT THING LOOMS UP

like Campbell's "Who Goes There" Jim Arness tall as Olson inside a
rubberglove suit tears the door off an arctic station where Scientists
confront alien life & fall apart in the impossibility (the impassability)
of the Other, the Thing

The Beat Thing hulks back recalled by reductivist historians & true-
believing fans obsessed hermeneuticists who get everything but the
Thing itself who rages off like Frankenstein's doppleganger ripping up
trees & crunching freeways into cement accordions

A Bomb denied at Smithsonian & Shoah in doubt or erased into
Schindler's kitsch what kind of history can Beat receive? what was
revolutionary life like on a daily basis? what kind of jobs bought time
to ruminate on one's alienation? who raised the kids? who walked the
dog? these were oppositional communities expressing & embodying
values unified by ideological & spiritual codes around the clock,
supporting reinforcing poets & artists in epiphanies, ecstasies as well
as tending to the fallen

•

ka-chung

Beat ephemera fills up shoeboxes mice nest in

Beat lounge acts at Ramada Inn bars near airports

9

Beat cruise mingle w/ Beat survivors sit at Captain's table w/ *poete du jour* & dance to elderly bebop band at night win costume-contest feed sharks masterpieces harpoon beached wails have a bunch of books signed by blind bard riffing disenchanties adored singing up from the waxed floor his high led to

Beat correspondence school ads on TV John Saxon reads off the course offerings

Beat fairs rent space w/ tables of books, berets, records, leotards, videocassettes, CDs, posters, 8 x 10 glossies, period antiquities in bakelite, chrome, tigerskin pincushion vinyl, pushbutton cherry gizmos, classic Tupperware in stacks (it's really the looks not the books)

Beat things shrink inside outsize sweaters wedge into room corners away from lone candle jammed in wax caked wine bottle; Beat gamins & Jack Spratt *artistes* shade-goggled eyes above black turtleneck rims

Beat wax museums in Fisherman's Wharf downtown Lowell McDougal Street & Beat Thing Hall of Fame wing of Planet Hollywood on Sunset Boulevard

•

Beat leftovers second-stringers impersonators at Beat fests & contests for the best Kerouac & Burroughs while in another hotel Elvises spangle glitter lip curl compete for credibility

Beat kareoke franchises

Beat Generation (the musical) touring show at burb malls & civic centers; Beat 900 numbers for phone bop prosody or Mamie Van Doren clone phone sex bongo

Beat flesh pixeled jigsaw bricolage CD Roms; Beat DNA flash-frozen sperm & eggs at Better Baby Boutiques new stock added weekly as oldtimers give it up before drying up

•

Beat bulk lurch to lunch through plateglass posh chez cafe doors pour blood over crisp white linen tablecloths fans magic act away for wall hangings

Beat thing headbutts into corporate conference room where suits hold out pens for him to marathon grab as he signs contract after contract stacks up a big deal

the agent Charlie McCarthy's a propped up Beat body against press conference wall

Beat superstar on MTV fastcut scratch 50s newsreel footage intercut w/ sitcom knows best voices over Kurt Loder asks Burroughs about killing his wife

Beat CEO of media congealment spars w/ Bill Gates in razor-sharp khakis & Italian soft leather loafers for global ownership of poetry on Charlie Rose

Beat creature from black lagoon dips spoon into tub of Ben & Jerry
Kerouac Carmel Walnut Chunk Satori

Beat nix sticks pen into toxic state of inc (orporation) to finish epic PR
for Disney Beatsville urban mall themepark

Beat infomercial Anne Waldman hosting looks cool in new do & black
silk sheath & stockings insouciant red beret w/ Beat bodyguards
Ginsberg Burroughs on each side of the overlit divan

Beat tour jackets T-shirts numbered prints of Beat photos by Redl Stoll
McDarrah framed offered round the clock on Beat shopping channel

Beat Gap line of chinos lumberjack flannel shirts Dr. Dean beat shades
Joe Camel unfiltered beat smokes Armani blue black basement zoots
to suit up in & walk down to theme bar restaurant Coolsville chain
owned by three publishers owned by a transglobal media conglomer-
ate owned by a network of oil companies owned by a consortium of
arms dealers owned by a clot of drug producers owned by a massive
webwork of Swiss bankers & German brokers in silent partnership
with Japanese alchemists in collusion with Chinese gerontologists as
proxies for Reverend Moon

Beat mercenary high steppers bottom feeders set up emporia marts in
college towns & fast food dance halls troughs underwrit by Dr.
Pepper's new beat cola & MacDonald's beat meat subs espresso shakes
Bongo Burgers Cool Slaw

Beat cross country tours in refurbished Chevys & fintailed Caddies
driven by fast-talking clean-cut Neal-like tour guides who park at neo-

beat motels stapled along 66 w/ bar jukeboxes stocked w/ bop rhythm 'n' blues & haiku cocktail napkins

Beat Blockbuster shelves filled w/ old & new A & B Hollywood beat flicks plus full stock of alternative beat video readings performances of survivor beats sub-beats micro-beats in Xerox wrapper hand-lettered plastic cases along w/ second & third generation beat-identified groups performers & momentarily cool souls

Beat motif lap dancers beret-ribbed rubbers XXX loops gay road buddies XXX dildoes rebel leather flight jackets slave jeans w/ snap open back flap for bongo beat fisting

Beat outfits w/ gold leaf Burroughs signature on barrel, HH monogrammed smack baggies, Gallo special edition Thunderbird label reproduces page from *On The Road* scroll comes in cases of 24 poorboy screwtop bottles & isn't sold downtown, Cassady nickel & dime bags w/ mini silkscreen photo of Neil in white T-shirt & deluxe kilo limited silkscreened last photo of Neil on tightrope walking railroad tracks somewhere in Mexico numbered & signed by Kesey, bonus presentation set of gold bullets in brass plaque plush lined case w/ certificate of authenticity numbered & signed by William Lee

•

Beat babies bop to new digital old sounds still new to geezer beats yanked back to youngsville at first spine of night groove Bird Miles Bud Monk Max Klook Diz Ming sit up day & night CD after CD of Benedetti's direct-to-disc acetates & paperbacked tapes of Bird choruses weave into time's sandstorm

Beat babies slip into beat threads hip-hop to Blakey Messenger riffs thrum medium trance imagine style a 8-by-10 glossy backlit *flaneur* underworld link to scrapbook legacy tradition of cool & hip snapping fingertips muffed in smack silk fuck you square block power constipated statues shadows groovers move in & out of offbeat click of Zippo lighter cook up resist split

Beat babies sample 50s clip art icon of remote past plastic pliestocene Zippy Sunday strip says "Let's Pretend It's 1996" Winston Smith Tom Tomorrow *detournement* of roses prick wil-hold appearances of a more organized repression celebrating safe passage out of the Depression & W W 2 ("the Big One" Dobie's dad endlessly reiterated to blank bleach white blond son & deer-panic pal Maynard G.)

Beat babies babble homosocial anarchism in short-thread bars & coffe houses & tuned in standard issue lumberjack plaid shirts black 'Frisco jeans righteous against the state of everything the state's got to state

Beat Notre Dame City Lights pews vibrate w/ seekers reading selves into being & nothingness from bookshelves of recent classics luminous array rack after rack candybars impulse buy for change any change you got

Beat babies flow stealth cool wanna be free wear baubles avoid foibles go east to Buddha cushion & fortune cookie satori drink black milk of pop cult gift continent part of the global economy colony washed white

Beat babies clueless duesless bluesless desolate nevertheless

•

Beat boom
Beat room for boon
Beat loom to weave yarns
Beat doom to deceive belief
Beat tombs for paying devotees only
Beat wombs & sperm banks
Beat gloom perfume sampler inside GQ
Beat Zoom benny soda in a can
Beat moon over beat oasis on Sunset Boulevard
Beat noontime rhyme fest in downtown plaza
Beat tunes K-Tel sells on late night TV
Beat runes of living & dead writer warriors embossed in
leather made in Taiwan bookmarks sold at Barnes &
Nobles checkout counters
Beat loons blueing dusk crying flight
Beat buffoon loops remembering youth
Beat spittoons U.S. roadmap intaglio on beat bar woodfloor
Beat octaroons all claiming kinship to Bird or Bob Kaufman
Beat platoons in formation kick up their Capesios on stage
at Radio City Music Hall

•

beat me w/ beets red beets white beets deep dark vein blue beets beat
me up & down uptown & downtown
beat me daddy eight to the bar
beat me momma with beret stuffed barbells
beat me reet me tear me up shred my snowflakes up into the sky

beat me bash me break me put me back together again
in stamped-out beat demigod saltshakers
beat me w/ leatherwing bats wing moth flutter stutter
beat me repeat me repeal me heal the hole in the line to

keep the flow circulating onward
beat me in history sleep pools
baby shoes are bronzed in
beat me in goldleaf halo spike
lamb ascent into nosebleed ether ringing altitude
beat me down into black rabbi beanie ink wink
beat me up into shaman fright mask asking really tough
essential questions
beat me through to Zen insouciant teleport satori epiphany
pillow to rest my wearies
beat me into Max's bass drum foot pedal thump bomb thump
beat me out of Bird's brass articulate waterfall sass & jazz
& urgent jive emergency of thee I sing
beats me what it means to be beat to retreat from
onward pulse dead on arrival hell no
beats me
beats you
beats us

●

hey
I don't wanna be civilized
don't wanna be tiny-towned into little plastical citizen

pink lucite letter opener & bill-payer bobalink
chirper of microchippy song of complicity

don't wanna be smooth like uh good manners
at gut knot status trough benevolence where all of me
's malevolent, my lips Elvis-up meat cushion curtains
into hand-biting funky uncapped teeth going underneath
upper dermis into hot lava core rough stuff
'nuf said

don't wanna be tamed or maimed by the taming
into pet poet monkey at honkie hoky pokies
uh uh not gonna be low-key modal Windham Hill
not up for grabs not buying in not selling out
want a million dollars want the Millionaire
J. Berseford Tipton of Publishers Clearing House
to bring a camera crew to my bumpy door
knock loud because there's no doorbell
& I'll be there to take the check & bow
to Candid Camera w/ a flash of rat glamor glee

don't wanna be forgotten but don't wanna be remembered
in rememberings' dismembering

don't wanna be polite in politic of conspicuous display want to be
forthright not necessarily right

don't wanna be beat or hip or cool or way ironic & get stuck in the
tonic rut

•

beat amnesia synethesia wrinkled pillowcase neuron
walnut blood cased in bone shell bowl topped by black beret in black
sock mask smoke leaks out of

beat aphasia neuro logic defunct

beat miasma plasma lay low on bloodbank gurney

beat infinitesimal dismal schmaltz spew to tender pinks of fantasy
landers looking for a home some roots a rind of lineage to pillage

beat static attack attic barracuda scholars dealers collectors scavenge
commandos elbow through handblown windows
to get at rummage life sale boxes of books letters & knickknacks

beat vatic battery of drummers & commissary working on commission
tube suction vacuum laterals into collapsed veins & torment stains
once brains

beat erratic attempts at negotiating uniqueness from form fitting
Velcro Spandex ex-ecstatic turnaround now ordinary wheeler dealer
whiner against what rolled by without him
beat guy goggled by gone blue & yellow filtered shades lurches out of
incense church of bud into civilian dutiful everyone's-a-cop boulevard,
a hard yard to bird

•

Beat Thing Tromar film fest

Beat Thing Marvel comicbook where the Hulk goes soft & turns to
poetry & estrangement gets engaged to a Beat chick whose father's in
development & mamma's an heiress & everyone's used to sudden
transformations

Beat Thing mannequins in better store windows everywhere haut
couture rebeats & junkie Dacchau haunted hunted models skip down
runways in flashbulb
cascade fireworks

Beat Thing twang 50s metallic speckled Fender solidbody guitars in
pink & charcoal, special Les Paul beat Deluxe
limited issue w/ chartreuse fingerboard, reissue Korla Pandit B-3 organ
ringed in neon tubing

Beat Thing sewed together like a baseball knocks on the door selling
poems for food like Lindsay in the 20s but nobody's home

Beat Thing solid pure Bakelite busts of Jack Neil Allen & Bill you can
weigh your manuscripts down with or put in a pantheon row on
Beethoven knickknack shelf

Beat Thing serial killer movies unstoppable blade scythes through
Levittown mows down squares rapid fire their bodies stack up like
cords of wood

Beat Thing singalong kapplemeister a one a two Mitch Miller cool
goatee extending small chin from maestro prow

Beat Thing ducks one liners & machinegun Lenny Bruce compassion
rage gets out of the line of fire offstage away from firing's range

Beat Thing's early addiction to Muzak sets stage for trance music
minimalism rave techno; Beat Thing's early gloss of Dos Passos
sampling leads way for hiphop; Beat Thing's fuck you inspires punk
safetypinned up yours as it gets deturned by Situationists; Beat Thing's
public poetry picked up by rock 'n' roll churchgoers & later by perfor-
mance poets mixing & matching everything TV failed to do; Beat
Thing's wings helicopter its bunched rejects to perfection of rejection;
Beat Thing's defection infects others throughout & beyond its time

•

beat's moot, a tomb
beat's mood, doom
even a beat snood
holds jello brains together

beat's through, a trough
zookeeper's snorkle into

beat's elapsed, collapsed
its time's run out the no exit door
into backward streets of kitsch
& socialist realist hero statues
& retroactive sales of books & other stuff

beat's dead, 'nuff said
it's rotting in the tool shed with Dada

& mamma bear despair *surrealisme*
a stink in time smells sweet
ready to spread on old ground
plant new seedlings new weeds
stir the wet trap poetry gets clapped w/in
get real, beat's a done deal

•

Start a new world a new day buy a two-bit bag of biscotti at Green
Street Italian bakery, then get free coffee from poet counterman Bob
Stock at the Co-Existence Bagel Shop:

Chris Maclaine in sporty tweed cap speeds into audio range w/ hipster
murmurs to the Bellsons already there; the Vignes (Dion & Lorelei)
frazzle in their sizzle against the wall, something's going down; Mike
Nathan, Bobby Fischer of painting, ambles in, twitchy laugh, hair
scythe cleaves face; Hube the Cube's reads the morning *Chronicle* in
yet another new orbit of comic chemic roulette, cigarettesmoke turns
his beard into redwood; hungover Tom Albright croaks significance to
Irene Taverner, Bird's U.K. penpal; Paddy O'Sullivan gums croissant,
silk cape frayed, tricorner hat smashed, its plume bent; Patricia Marx
blue eyes you don't lie to, she said "I want to kiss you to see how it
feels," an experiment, eros empirically shopping; Lyle Tollefson skids
in w/ Leonard Hull hatching another put-on maybe this time on the
Muni; Kaufman bent out of shape after a couple of nights in a holding
tank worked over by Bigarini; Micheline pisses beer on Green Street
corner; across the street the Duncan-Spicer contingency w/ Joanne &
Nemi drawing the boys upward & out; Bad Talkin' Charlie Dawkins
carving fetishes; Joe Overstreet w/ a stack of sketches under his arms;

Manuel Neri & Pete Farakis in their basement studio under Trieste, big action paintings blaze against cement walls & papier-mache scultures of humans & animals all over the place, KJAZ loud echo; Bob Alexander on the upswing, shaved head, black horn-rimmed glasses, leather wristband, doesn't miss a thing; Jay Bagel wearily counting the receipts; Leo Krekorian serves beer to noon beats at The Place; Linda Lovely turns any room into a Speed Graphic freeze-frame panoramic photo; Cowboy finally parks the slowest heap on the planet & ambles out, horn in bag, exhaling; Eric Nord's got two underage chicks on his large lap; Father Pierre descends from Bread & Wine Mission to bless his parish; Victor Wong does espresso then crosses Columbus into Chinatown whistling "Donna Lee"; Bob Marquese bebop bassplaying sadsack Eyore; Don Graham, full beard, draped in large trenchcoat, paces, hands behind back, in Discovery,then kneads his face, his beard, talking of Agape & Eros, Dostoevsky, Neihbur, Kierkegaard; Sandy, Don Martin's chick, sexpot combat cookie, chews on my ear in Washington Square Park; Bill Weisjahn (piano), Max Hartstein (bass), Frank Phipps (valve trombone), Sonny Nelson (drums), sometimes Leo Wright (alto, flute), house-band at The Jazz Cellar & Carla Bley's squeezing through the narrows with drinks on a tray, Bob Briggs behind the bar; Matt Vidaver's suave intelligence & irk; Guy Wernham (poet, translator, writer, Red) bartender at the Anxious Asp, chewing on cigarette holder w/ red punkt burning butt; Miss Smith's Tea Room before there was a Coffee Gallery; Shig in the City Lights turret; LeBlanc fresh from a NY ad agency divesting all for Tao; Mad Marie between giggles reminds us of her Mafia connections; Swanson walked off Nord's party pad roof happily oblivious to swan songs; conga wizard Milt in between shifts washing dishes; Lasnier hammered the silver of our full circle; Henri Lenoir, continental maestro of Vesuvio's, a letch enchanter in black beret, teeth clenched

(Left to right) Juanita Dixon, Robert Alexander, Wallace Berman, Shirley Berman on Speedway Avenue, Venice California, 1958. *Photograph by Charles Brittin*

on dark wood burl cigarette holder; Bob Seider, porkpie hat, lazy loaded eyes, blows sleepy "All of Me" at Bop City dawn jam; David Rafael Wang, caped, looking for Sherry Martinelli for Pound takes; John Chance throws three pennies on the table for my first I-Ching read-out; Ju Ju corners Weiners for signifying in Wentley; Nemi Frost soft creamy round body, Chanel, turpentine; Lee & idell in Portrero hill pad, grass hermetic yoga, all its devotees instant statues; shark smooth Lenny Monroe's sportscar pulls up to the Bagel Shop door looking to score; Don Crawford's pad above the pasta factory, upright bass & banjo, jazz on the hi-fi; nomads from the East coast frequent as mail; Bremser upstairs at The Place, talking hip bop, cigarette on lip like Garfield; Perkoff in front of City Lights talking variable foot while Friday night traffic pours up & down Columbus; Lenore & Lew at East/ West House chop ginger & scallions to throw into the mix; not amused, Brautigan storks up against a bar wall peering down through cloudy wire-rims; Joe Dunn stacks a new White Rabbit book fresh out of Greyhound downtown mimeograph machine; Larry Jordan, a tall whisper, brings another batch of hand-made Ivans to City Lights basement; Allen Deinstag's tight curly hair & intense gopher gaze; Whalen buys second-hand music, Bach, Telleman, & sets out to look for someone with a piano; Snyder's leg in a cast, drinking a beer, en route to another mountain; Ferlinghetti's startled impenetrable blue eyes; LaVigne's suite of ink drawings, a flower dying through a long night; Joan Brown's round blue eyes & porcelain doll Harry Langdon mouth alive in the dawn after an all-nighter; back to Chris Maclaine, meth propelled, in travel agency doorway blowing old Scot lament on bagpipe mouthpiece

•

fans & groupies, scene guppies
feast on folly's debris while snails suck up
cast-off shit & assorted haste-dropped waste

nose into musk crotch of aura fame
digits dent hero flesh for ripeness

William & Joan Brown, 1957 *Photograph by C.R. Snyder*

hype ripens to rot open foul lotus
decay musk hooks devotee into crawling
around on hands & knees to please

•

the beat thing beaten down into a thin strip of laser repelling bar-code
the beat thing smashed flat bread dough
the beat thing inflated w/ nitrous oxide muzzle making cosmic &
mundane giggle cacophony at the symphony

•

crushed beercan disc necklace lei
around conga player's thick neck rocket

bras busting through red cashmere cuffed
Levis taut T-shirts smoking gun & butt 50s
lurid paperback rearrange war shadows
curl around Louis Jordan shuffle time Lindy
pulse sock bop pinwheel joint too wet for kicks
passed around by some chick tricks her baffled cat w/ quotes from de
Beauvoir's Galouise sandblasts lungs implode his load bunched ribbed
jockstrap rap draft
condom Korea read Baghavad-Gita Signet Maya's
chill nets catch kid butterfly on the sly

·

What about Beat food?
Was there a special cuisine or was it eat & run or hit Chinatown for
War Won Ton or rice congee at Sam Wo's dodging velocity of waiter
Edsel Fong's wired humiliations & verbal aggression at roundeyed
hipsters & tourists dragging in smoky frames for rehab or Green
Valley family style meals in echo chamber
linoleum vault plastic ivy creeping over faux
wine grille bricabric ceiling grate or deep grease
garlic bread Spaghetti Factory wicker bowl of starch
to soak Anchor Steam saturate carafes of red wine castanets at
flamenco floorshow or mooncakes
thick suet gut paste or bagfuls of hazelnut biscotti
or tubfulls of fried onionrings at Mel's Drive-In
after it's all over the bar's closed need flight fuel
or yosenabe in J-Town slurped with sake & constant
wisdom burning the air between us or North Beach
sourdough fresh from the bakery oven before light

breaks night off like smoking memory hunk or all
the awful great fried breaded brains smog air & layer
oilslick of morning mouth clothing stinks of after
& we ice nostrils with powders make us talk louder
& longer crave sushi especially wasabe bullet train
blasting eyes into inland seas of kelp hurricane weep
or shrimp cocktails at Swan Oyster Depot on Polk
dip pink volt into red horseradish tomato karma lemon
after rye toast soaked in Blum's sweet butter or linguine
dreamy shimmer glazed with green Pesto paste shiny
at family-style dive long tables raw red in recycled bottles
throttle adam's apple w/ laser precise burn through olive
oil veneer or ketchup drowned fries Jaunita's crowned
with pepper black & white bite to soak up tequila shots
lime & salt open tongue's edgy ridges or a parade of
Martinis at Vesuvio's getting Ollie to load the toothpick
w/ shishkabob of olives & onions w/ LeBlanc waiting to
carry me home to Tina who reminds me for weeks how
lousy I am w/ liquor or after-gig pizzas at Sorrento's
or questing for kosher dills at David's or chewing steak
wallets at Tad's w/ stuffed potatos erupting green onion
carpets of steam table redlights or Mike's Pool Hall
minestrone at the bar w/ Nureyev in trenchcoat
& the sharp blur backdrop of pool hustlers rustling
tourist marks or crunch sawdust crackers stuck w/ tough brie at
gallery openings balance acrid white wine in plastic cup or ardently
overcooked chile sludge leaking out of
rubbery tortillas at potluck party in a basement car
wheels hum overhead & beatniks slump into black
wallpaper spackled w/ splatter of red lights & pot

luck spine tuningfork jazz maybe Monk or Twardzik
or machine slicing thick cornbeef yellowfat edged slabs on corn rye for
George & Polly at the Berkeley Bagel or tofu cubes float in miso fog up
glasses or down at the Wharf w/ Judy J scarfing calamari or bologna
discs slapped between Wonder Bread glued shut w/ mayonnaise
or desert mudpies you always rolled your eyes before
digging in or baked salmon at the Roscoe's Bastille Day
feast or fasting in white walled flat or ground round steak tartar we ate
in life w/out a hotplate & no care about spasms of microorganisms or
stew up at Jules' while he was at work & we were at work smirching
his bed before he threw you out into my arms or cold raw red potatoes
sprinkled w/ Vegesal or sourdough cubes dunked into fondue sludge
smudged w/ green eyelashes of dill or
bowls of bar popcorn & beer in the afternoon look out
the window at tourists furtive up & down Grant Avenue or
tostadas & chile rellenos in Mission tacqueria late at night
when mariachi trio walk down narrow aisle breaking hearts
or Sabicas enters La Bodega camelhair overcoat draped over his
shoulders while we stuff our faces w/ paella or into Adelle's Let's Eat
Right to Keep Fit book of revelations revamp our rations go wheat
germ brewer's yeast blackstrap molasses Tiger's Milk chinquapin honey
from Farmer's Market organic soyburgers feel surge of immortality
turn beatnik skins inside out or feast of pickled herring eaten out of
the jar boosted from Safeway or
Rand's Roundup in L.A. where hungry wolfish writers ate all-you-can-
eat for $1.99 or square-shaped burgers filled w/ breadchunks & onions
fit just right on white bread ketchup-soaked w/ pickle mandalas or
grill-tormented American Cheese sandwich you need Lava Soap to
grind off grease sutured hands or back in the Apple bringing a bag of
hot Planter's goobers (a quarter of a pound for a quarter) to Artie &

John Reed, Los Angeles, late '50s. *Photograph by Charles Brittin*

Betty's pad & listen to Al & Zoot records & smoke Bronx brown weed
or Stockwell treats me to a Chef's Salad in Hollywood burger bunker
or Keinholz buys me a Caesar Salad at Barney's Beanery or harvesting
Ralph's dumpster cornucopia of fruits & vegetables dumped there
nightly for the slightest imperfection or hotplate veggie broth cube in
tin cup or seeing how much a teabag can be reused or infusing an
orange Charm in a glass of water or organic sunflower seeds in shells
spitting husks into a metal wastebasket & writing haiku while rain
rivets the tarpaper shed roof w/ added water percussion from leaks
into an old paintcan or
early morning coffee & English muffin in Market Street Woolworth's
watching shortorder cook Nijinsky stay in one place & be everywhere

flipping flapjacks sunnyside up eggs rippling crackle of bacon strips
hiss of hashbrown potatoes hits the grill or first crab of the season at
open air steam cart at the Wharf or a bowl of Grape Nuts rising
pyramid out of Pet Milk or Lee Romero springing for chile rellenos or
oysters shimmering in lemonjuice w/ auras of pearl shell & a bowl of
white sawdust crackers dipped into horseradish or 7th Day Adventist
veggie burgers at stand off Market near the Protestant Bookshop which
years later is taken over by Scientologists or huge white oval plate of
sashimi from the Tokyo Fish Market & sake shared w/ Bob & Linda
Hawkins at our Jones Street pad or a Deaf Smith organic peanutbutter
sandwich on wholewheat home-made bread for Clark only to have
him recoil & confess goober allergy or Thanksgiving Larkin Street
turkey Tina basted in vin rose in first trimester of pregnancy & puked
all during dinner & never drank rose again or dinner at the McClure's
pad on Fillmore of k-ration food bought at Army/Navy surplus store or
pot cake heavy w/ nutmeg & ginger washed down w/ black coffee
laced w/ cheap brandy or breaking off a hunk of carob candy or
mashing soybeans into soyburgers popped into fryingpan greased w/
saffola oil or dinner at Gravenites' watching "The Godfather" on
KRON-TV or peeling off tangerine skin whose oil made our hands
smell of it all night long or house sitting for the Schiffrins in Silver
Lake eating everything & anything in the fridge on the shelves all the
veined & moldy cheeses even a jar of capers or frozen Heath Bars we'd
eat at Polk Street Royal movie theater crunching through "Hard Day's
Night" & "Sayonara" or mushrooms stuffed w/ garlic & parsley fried
in butter w/ a splash of olive oil or eating grilled halibut at Tadich's as
Carol's date & going through downtown afternoon ithyphallic through
the tunnel to Larkin Street monk space for lovemaking on Norman's
surplus cot or L.A.'s poor poet horsemeat fillets or first orange peppery

hit of nasturtiums blazing on cushions of oil-slicked spinach or
endless onion dips at openings & book parties or tunafish casseroles
or meatloaf for nights until it got rubbery like jerky or grilled
American Cheese sandwiches or Ritz Crackers salty straw in toked-out
mouths unable to sing cool clear water or sour upchuck baby milk soft
Monterey cheese cheap from Doug's dairy or cheapo tins of sardines
mashed between limp Graham crackers after the redbird wore off or
baked garlic cloves zit squeezed onto sourdough sponges or chive
colonized soupy eggsalad drools out of finger-dented white bread onto
chambray shirtfront or nutmeg eggnog hip square Christmas party pad
& everyone wants to be home again
or Bastille Day baked salmon for boojy Bohemians gone middleaged &
nostalgic or solo amble down Columbus Avenue walking to work
munching cheapo peanut brittle or Tina's hand-decorated hardboiled
egg paradox of loss & gain in my paper lunchbag or sprinkle salt out
of aluminum shaker onto knish held in waxpaper in lower East Side
ghetto of my forebears or times when anything in the mouth works
whether it's crumbs off the floor or suck on paper just to chew as if
eating food or stand in line decades later at Chez Beat prix fixee grub
dressed up to false teeth roots no longer connected to want or food not
bombs or food not tombs or latkes at Halsey's at a New Year's party
nobody else attended or watch Abbot & Costello at the Rugby
chewing Jujubes or drinking massive daiquiris at La Rondella with
Diane, Robert, McNaughton, Oppen in & out of Alzheimer's telling us
about Pound or
fries in red plastic basket at Clown Alley in vortex of meth heads
rebuild every square inch of utopia all over again & again or
eating stops when everything inside is blocked
& she sucks on ice-cubes to stay alive

•

okay what was poetry & jazz all about? how was it done, who did it, did it really make it, why? Nobody knows its origins — claiming to be its progenitor, Rexroth says he did it in Chicago w/ Jelly Roll in the late 20s early 30s — ruth weiss claims to have started it in 1946 in New Orleans — Vachel Lindsay in the 20s "boomalay boomalay" "Daniel Jazz" — scanners say it started in the caves moving across *shir ha-sharim* Bible plains into qawalli singing Sufis fanning gutstrings duende cante troubadour courts into Brit balladeers across winter drifts to Schoenberg's *sprachstimme* & Louis Armstrong's amnesia inspired glossolalia — Edith Sitwell ratatat *Facade* Walton's teadance jazz band hotcha — from Africa West to Delta South to Broadway Hart Gershwin — Langston Hughes in Jazz Age Harlem club — Duke's recitatives — Babs Gonsalves Leo Watson Slim Gaillard putty putty — Little Walter Robert Johnson Blind Willie McTell — where does it start or end in the music of the words in the words beyond words — jazz itself & what surrounds it — abiding community of devotees w/ or w/out goatees — to whites jazz was a way out into black as white was black jazz's way in — its instruments scales rhythms harmonies — no confusion — subversive celebratory fusion — oompah-pah state instruments square note hymnody church & state strut tripped between beat & offbeat catch spirits & let loose in-spiriting bodies — found music of language in the language of music — Mad TV's beat poet hawks coffeebean heart attack breakfast cereal — parody's the melody of history taking itself seriously — "This Is An Orchestra" Stan Kenton's outstretched arms mouths Steinberg scrawl code balloons in big lumpy Guston clouds gloom out of his matinee idol grey at the temples rat fratz — Spike Jones Mickey Katz Homer & Jethro Beat poets — "John and Marsha" Stan Freeberg prescient

minimal pomo performance art — Laurence Harvey reads Thomas
Benton "This Is My Beloved" on Ertugen produced Atlantic disc —
Screamin' Jay Hawkins' "I Put A Spell On You" — not Rexroth clunk
recite you killed him you sonsabitches in your etcetera gray flannel
suits dutifully backed up by the Cellar Jazz Quintet — not even
Richard Lord Buckley's Barrymore hipster rolled gold who sounds like
Ezra Pound trilling his rrs poetica — yes to Lenny Bruce jewboy yes to
Jack Kerouac lumberjack knew what others didn't about swinging —
Ken Nordine's Hammond B-3 voice could be selling Chevrolets —
Jean Shepherd reclaiming Robert Service — grain of voice — intent
— *duende* — whatever you say jim as long as it jams — Baraka rocks
& nails fools w/ song that won't be wronged —

•

beat beaten beat up on the off the beat
battered buttered buffed
beats me
beat it

•

not only black but red gel light from above
from below turning anomie into monstrosity
not only red but khaki WW2 surplus Korean castoffs
not only khaki but earth colors in general
marginality seeks camouflage no matter how
uniform it gets it's a vanishing cream a dream
of flow & flux unnoticed through all specifics
not only earth colors but florid red lipstick

powder white face & black eyeliner defines times
not only florid red lacquer lipstick but tricks of
hair pulled back into a bun severe & remote
or unraveled rich foliage around her bohemian face
& ripe trace ether musk embrace of head space

•

Okay, what drugs did Beat Things do
unstoppable Golems clunk up Frisco hills &
crash through glass Nob Hill doors hit waxed tile floors bugged or
goofy prophets hex profit outreach for more upward agility
let me list the ways
wisdom sways through barroom doors
hardline juicers boozers lushes dipsos
unpeel *gemeinschaft* onion loops to steal
wise guy shifts in benny flipbook blur or
muggles giggles & pelvis wiggles sizzle
electric rootsystems light up epidermal cowl
dong bulb wired into cervical ark clutch
do redbirds sleepers newtime absinthe cafe blur
glazed out head down in a pool of dream drool
or nosedive into ether rag to regain the sky
flow through doors opening quicker than tics
or laser toke of opium tar brocades cocoon
or blade coke lines moon zoom cold precise
crater edges overburdened white light
into everything into everything else
or smack embalm your skin bongo
drum taut in freeze dry heat hit rush

wipe away clouds too loud your eyes
walled w/ shades fall in lay back land in Nod
or buttons boiled in aluminum pot on hotplate
eat every thorn drink up the soup & loop out
fight payphone octopus wires
get Bellevue to strap me down
or potcake chomped at Coffee Gallery
weary of Tina's definitive Jalapa trip blitz
which rewrote her itinerary or
ripped on Hollywood Boulevard bus en route to Silverlake
everybody knows I'm out of it & they're all stark narcs
behind shades I can't see through or
spiked punch electric surge flash flush
infusion of every never-ending nerve-end or
amT's scribe for canned Squibb prophecies
whose raw socket volcano rockets wisdom
uncoiled levels connect reassemble
scribble down what can't make sense in the morning
or first meth death Maclaine the poet piper kino eye
head spent flying hours scavenging brass doorknobs from Western
Addition demolition or Valo
inhalers boing microsecond infinite or paregoric
or bowel block Cheracol coughsyrup or
lung sandblast hashpipe hit & run into Sierra
Sound w/ Clark, J.P., Denny, & David to lay
heavy tracks through endless tunnel or wormless
tequila w/ Stephanie atop stacked highs
in redwood canyon ready to descend & start again
or painting Cameron's Scott Street flat w/ Army surplus
ether-based khaki paint rocket beyond Coleridge

to meet in tantric blur or popping buttons w/ Dean
 in his hungry Porsche grumbling to idell's idyll
through California hills to Riverside or in Jack
the Baptist's VW van to Isla Vista drinking
beer toking weed or 60's New Year's Eve
Nancy in aluminum foil dress smoke up
scale grass in Roscoe bathroom & downstairs
dance random hippie sway or all day
all night dexy writing monkey gibber
gargantuan nothing splatter of commas
& semicolons or tons of nutmeg cons grind
into gel caps for joint jump or knot guts
'shrooms twist through slime showrooms
shiny bloody brain furls slopped into chrome
trays or Hedricks' home brew knocked flat back
on bathroom tilefloor fixed on ceiling mazda or
hurl in trunk of farewell party or Dino spike
smoke funnel kiss lung puncture blast off or
buzzed Crosby on Van Damme topdeck sings
Beatles to David & Tina below or achingly
clear blow-torqued bluegrass livingroom session w/ Greg
or Mount Rushmore heads in Romero's Portrero
pad & Angel LP Yehudi explains ragas Ravi
Shankar unravels our spines or February birthday
for Artie WB & me ozoned on floor watch
Magnificent Ambersons Larry Jordan projects onto
fold-out screen or Jim Hall/Red Mitchell at Keystone
while I nod out between bars Chris is alert or
drive a car one eye open & another eye shut or
dive w/ snorkel into cocaine Himalayas or do

Ali Baba hookah bubble pipe on foam-filled pillow
or day/night speed through the Apple's allures to home
& feel warm sleep cement inch up from toes fill rills & ruts of busy
buzzy brain brings erase & jazz on the radio or Larkin Street deep flu
fever a flask of cognac lacquers
or Sturdy tripping at Coffee & Confusion gets our music really gets
into it or T & me reenter & roulette restless
LPs on the phono & wind up weeping to worn 10" Pete Seeger LP
driven by unstandard time heart waver voice or
at Black Hawk with the Halseys waiting for Monk's set
or it could go on w/ Fentanyl patches IV insert new drip
protein into catheter click whir plugged-in pump or
short-circuit Ativan planchettes your ballpoint message dream knot
maze tangled baby scrawl or more liquid morphine sucked out of clear
plastic dose-measured tube
& sleep

•

Redl's photo of David & Tina in Filbert St. alleyway
w/ Bevan gets to all who see it who know us
or knew us or were there or now
in their beginning know our end
we all have young photos to look forward to

•

yes cast off once fresh flesh for old corduroy folds
yes letch leech & strut at Beat fests w/ young believers
yes males or females or transmutants

radiate halo of holy moly been there

yes give em myth light w/out sunblocker

yes everyone knew Jack

yes of course we know Allen

yes Neil sold me lids & Bill palmed me bags

yes sign more remnants for crypt keeper Kush

yes spontaneous bop prosody in sweatshop doorway

yes am rude & seek company w/ rowdy loud disruptives

yes in deep sympathy unrelated to manners

not to the manor borne instead both fan & fox

stalk & trot through library chickencoop

yes hiked w/ Gary through North Beach who showed me

what concrete splitting green energy to eat

yes shilled for Lew's snooker gambles

yes bought blow from Michael we sampled

like movie deals in broad daylight car

yes gave Allen a white coffecup to puke in

he being nude at the party wanted everyone

naked in his hands or mouth or ass

yes Creeley wanted to punch me out

in the kitchen at the Big O Berkeley party

but then forgot what for

yes Roshi Phil couldn't stop the giggles

& Ferlinghetti said poetry was over

& went back to painting figures

go figure

yes comrade Micheline shamed them

as did Corso made them roll their eyes

try to apologize

yes Rexroth's rump on the chaise said goodnight

yes Lamantia's cape & rapture & old world arcana
yes Kirby Doyle's tall Raskolnikov overcoat
yes Michael's black Frisco jeans & blue hawks
yes Joanne's blonde ferocious Buddha dharma
fell into place in fresh picked flowers in
special treasure from the Journey to the East
yes Lenore was an olive grove whose oil
slick made lesser cats spin out speeding
yes what do you want to know
now that we are nowhere to be seen
as you see us & are as you are living
dying process flow to nowhere
flux to somewhere where
weight of past secretes in pancreas
undoes secrets & lives in legend photographs
& can't move past its past
media raw ore for kids to adore
yes Olson was giant inhaler
huge gut gargantuan liver
like Duncan was ever curious &
constant in arts & acts of connecting
w/ tempered hopefulness
yes poetry baffles ambition
negates sedition disallows perdition
guides the scan sweep Dante frenzy
retrieves what's imagined & conceives what's not
yes Creeley was/is handsome intense eye to glass
lyric cannabis bliss giddy seriousness
yes Wieners wherever he wrote was right
& in poetry's deep core rite & Jack

knew what it was all about & chose to
die for love's lack & death's deal stacked
& fixed each card nicked or bent for touch
the mechanic's skill wills future tricks
yes Leroi Jones Emperor of the era
yes David Rafael Wang
yes John Chance toss of 3 Chinese coins
yes John Allen Ryan's nicotine goatee
yes all those guys
all those disguises
eyes scan the bar & there's Spicer
Pruneface pure word Orpheus & yes
Lew Welch rises up from the floor to
reaffirm art of clarity in poetry
& poor Brautigan blonde stork in dark
Northwest mist had to turn the poem prose
yes Ferlinghetti
yes Gregorian chanting
yes Lamantia prodigy of scarves & rare
Egyptian fluids lace extasis formaldehyde
yes Brother Bill escaped cock Jimmy Stewart
quaver pump holy Eros on the loose
yes maitre Rexroth KPFA foghorn libertarian
Cleghorn generous & heroic yes
Ibn McNaughton son of suns of Black
Mountain spoons engraved deep care
despair for poetry's hopefulness
yes Patchen flat on his ass in Palo Alto
martyrologist prole prophet cocooned
yes Broughton winged kino eye brightness

John Weiners and Nemi Frost with two musicians from the house band,
Leo Wright and Frank Phipps —The Cellar, 1959. *Photograph by C.R. Snyder*

yes Don Schenker urgency between Stevens
& Williams & yes Ron Loewinsohn even then
in a suit & so many guys w/ or w/out ties
in poetry's monastery & Kaufman says no
to hypnogogic go-go & yes to abject magnets
yank streets into flux rage uncontainable
& radio sage Watts spins Zen in empire J.
Arthur Rank speak Buddha rolls forth
satori tractors level Marin onto encircled void
& yes Gavin Arthur mothballed silk sorcerer
robes of old Bohemian Club arts boyscouts
yes Harold Dull's scone pale poems
yes Lew Ellingham's sumptuous library cravat

sold piecemeal in vats to Discovery Roscoe
yes even Paddy O'Sullivan's hook & Cyrano plume
toothless spray weep not my children
yes Bob Stock's Portrero livingroom salon
where Weldon Kees ectoplasm silverfished
in & out of books stacked & stuffed in floor-
to-ceiling bookcases & yes Nancy Moore
moody verse talons for chicks poaching Brew
yes Daniel Moore illumined Ginsberg eyes
blew shenei & did dervish dance to Mecca
& back to Berkeley & Lee Romero's occult
inks on glass plate light show auras Goethe
chromatic in Topanga & the Fillmore
yes Creeley at State back from Mallorca
show & tell how measure marks time
space & how deep is love's ocean
yes devotional commotion
lotion of inner oils undulate rare odors
through skin's silk lining
yes Kerouac the lamb best w/ jazz
hipster outtakes & yes Leroi
wrested the music back home
yes Robert Duncan owl sage
jackdaw curious & deep sweep
yes lumberjack bards in plaid shirts
yes Stefan George silkwinged sprites
yes Stevensites & Elioteers fencing off
speech based rude boys from Paterson
& yes Berlitz sprung Yanks abroad like
Pound who went back from the new

while Bill went ahead & H.D.
finished 3 epics while her swains
couldn't & yes Kirby Doyle
jump-kicked hog peels out & down
Fillmore to score more meth to
make more poems & fix her gold
pink American beauty mouths
& moths lost in Allen's rabbi beard
yes Berrigan in 57th Street doorway
pounds bongos & knows exactly where
to go while Itkin elsewhere drowns in
Nightwood Judy Garland mash notes &
mythos & No-Doz & yes Cocteau's
Orphee & Le Sang
yes Langston outside rides
blue to white black riff runts &
Juju affronted disses John for
middle passage in Wentley & today on Valencia
run into Micheline w/ diabetes says
it doesn't get better no reprieve
Warner B flick Death Row con
moments before anonymous screw hand
pulls a switch & Coolidge edges the ledges
of shadow abyss in want of poem's heart
restored & yes McNaughton's heart
beats twice as fast & nothing lasts
& yes Joel Oppenheimer dailies & Blackburn precise
duende loaded dice roll out of play & yes
Clayton in vat cave deep like Cid instantly
responds to poetry & Baraka mourns Miles

Wallace Berman & Allen Ginsberg, Los Angeles, 1960. *Photograph by Charles Brittin*

death makes sons fathers no longer followers
who's left continues the fight & yes Jack
red scarf uplifts abject rejects castaways
from *techne's* refusal of entropy & yes
the usual redeye flight backwards to face future
as voidable nervefill stashed w/ old words
nostalgia & neuralgia old familiar aches & places
geezer warmup stasis approach death's oasis

•

who's beat now & then
who keeps score
who're the gatekeeper guys & gals who bar office doors
you need a password a look a book an agent &
good connections

BEAT THING: COMMENTARY

it was the Bomb
Shoah
it was void
spirit crisis disconnect
no subject but blank unrelenting
busted time
no future
suburban expand into past
present nuclear (get it) family
droids Pavlov minutiae
it was Jews w/ blues
reds nulled & jolted
Ethel & Julius brains smoke
pyre of shoes & eyeglasses
weeping black G.I.s
open Belsen gates
things are going to look different
when you get outside
understand that beforehand
 this book doesn't kid you
& don't forget the third effect
radioactivity, the power to shoot off
invisible atomic rays
even if the all clear's sounded
don't rush to leave the safe place
Geiger counts light leaks from ash

hand reaches up for your eyes
yes the atomic bomb is a terrible weapon
BUT not as terrible as most of us believe

Tillich tells us "it's the destiny of historical man
to be annihilated not by a cosmic event
but by the tensions in his own being & history" [1]

EIGHT SIMPLE RAID RULES:

ALWAYS shut windows and doors.
ALWAYS seek shelter.
ALWAYS drop flat on your stomach.
ALWAYS follow instructions.
NEVER look up.
NEVER rush outside after a bombing.
NEVER take chances with food or water.
NEVER start rumors. [2]

Furthermore, acquaintance with addicts proves that 'hypes' like being
'hypes.' They enjoy being a 'hype' as a hypochondriac enjoys being a
hypochondriac. They will argue that liquor affects people worse than
heroin, that drunks are often noisy and argumentative, while all a
'hype' wants is to be left alone. They dislike the social scorn, the
inconvenience of having to hide their addiction, but they enjoy the
effect of the drug, which keeps them from facing reality.
The juice of the poppy wrecks the body and warps the spirit. The life
of the addict is a living death. [3]

futureless clockface
Bulletin of Atomic Scientists pie-chart
Eternity black out
infinite unseen permutants
Hiroshima Maidens through
Saturday Review offices
shuffle bow hide mouth to Cousins
wrong & wronged *Fantastic Brain*
Destroyers "The testimony of a victim
will clinch the case against them
when they're brought to trail!"
"The house I live in, a plot of earth
a street, the grocer and the butcher
and the people that I meet;
the children in the playground,
the faces that I see;
all races, all religions,
that's America to me" sings Sinatra
in RKO backlot tenement

"A Kansas farmer, a Brooklyn sailor,
an Irish policeman, a Jewish tailor"
utopic plurality plastic lanyard
unity thongs for khaki G.I. nation hoods as
zootsuit jitterbug gold chain ceiling dancers
starlight all night razor & bullet flash
rationed gas & glamour
snooded riveters pitch in
to chance true romances
of misaligned diaphragm or
ancient Trojan pinhole burst

in backpocket wallet vault
dark backwards 4th of July
grope heat beneath cashmere
silk rayon buckle collage shields
stations of crossing over into her
nuclear August 13th rain of ruin
one bomb w/ 20,000 tons of TNT
evaporate mouth tongue ocean fun
red prong push back Levi pecker
form ache we sneak around parents
seek lava silk slippery finger smear
leaks out nylon rhythm crotch 'n' blues
Ruth Brown a humpty bumpty Louis
Jordan T-Bone Walker lindy magi
boogie chickerychick chala chala
"some of my best friends are Jews"
says Leni G.I. booted out of von
Ribbentrop's hill villa while Edward Waiter
Dachau's head shot himself
through the heart & lived to shoot himself
in the brain "He was a nice man, really"
said maid Gertrude of ex-boss Hitler
"of course he was mad"
"Claghorn's the name
Senator Claghorn, that is
ah'm from Dixie ah represent the South, son"
checkala romey in a bananika
ill at ease the little man said
some bread sir if you please
the waiter's voice roared down the hall

you gets no bread with ONE MEAT BALL!
movie swine sour kraut SS leather
skull pinups & power pimps smash up
Dana Andrew's defiant mug as
Great Artiste dumps bomb #2 on
second-choice Nagasaki at precisely
9:08 MacArthur stepped forward
removed a handful of fountainpens from
his pocket Werner Von Braun V-2
rocket wiz our guy on the range
cannibals all on the *Missouri*
always business as usual
population control & pesticides
Long Island kids grope out of DDT
bogs fog low flying cloud blankets
powder turns into oilslick evaporate
pocked skin pores German doctors watched
84 women react to their gas chamber death
"at first I thought it was simple lockjaw
a swelling in the back of the throat
light hemorrhages under skin
fever & a high pulse rate
rapid consumption of white blood
corpuscles, internal bleeding in
intestinal track" "stick-legged
starved bodies of European children
never smiled" "Census Bureau
reported last week nearly twice as many
U.S. citizens died of cancer during 1942-44
as were killed by enemy action in World War II"

"I am at present speaking less frequently
I have not been sleeping
I promise solemnly to the Almighty
the hour will strike when victory
will come to the Greater German Reich"
"If it is possible to outlaw the bomb
why not go the whole step &
outlaw war?"
"Two men
who don't trust each other
face each other
in a locked room, each
points a loaded machine gun at the other
one gun's a later model
no difference
whoever shoots first wins"
Picasso admired GI K rations
& Velvet tobacco rolled &
puffed by Stuart Little at
Ernie Pyle's funeral whose
chances were all used up
as cigarette shortage eased
"Yes, they're back"
Gimbels' sale of Army
DDT sprayers *Till the End*
of Time the biggest
noisiest New Year's Eve
bars open to dawn
stiff white shirt front back again for
chicks to lipstick write

General Patton fights for life w/
broken neck
auto accident en route to kraut field
pheasant shoot blood & guts
are we in time on time or out of it
college of cardinals on parade
red hat numero uno Archbishop
Francis Joseph Spellman of NY
Ray Milland lost weekend Anglo
Yank writer drunk marquis bosomy
Hazel Scott attained fame changing
Bach counterpoint into boogie woogie
"Mrs. Truman is the last lady" trumpets
Adam Clayton Powell Jr. contra DAR
earlier squirreled Marian Anderson
into programmatic darkness as UAW
Walter Reuther versus GM "They have
taken world millions they never toiled to earn
w/out our brain & muscle
not a single wheel could turn
we break their haughty power
gain our freedom when we learn
the union makes us strong"
"Kelly dances beautifully &
Sinatra sings the roof off"
Churchill Truman Stalin
gray trigger hairs at Potsdam
pulverized Mussolini hangs
upside down by his boots
Hitler's shoots a tunnel through his lobes

& FDR's brain hemorrhage implodes
Branch The Brain Rickey signs Jack
Roosevelt Robinson "unlike white
players he can't afford a day off" B-
25 crashes into Empire State's 78th & 79th floors kills 13
ink UN Charter's ratified
Robert Benchley's empty Algonquin chair
sugar shoe meat butter tire rationing ends
the year future ends
Kilroy was here
read the writing on the wall
I, The Jury Under The Volcano
A-Bomb tests at Bikini Atoll
Five full-color Kodachrome *National*
Geographic bright blue sky spread
fed aching crisp nuclear white fleece
spine disc clouds up into Amanita dome
page after page of eternity beauty
gorgeous end of time & future
Vive la France cries Pierre Laval
it lasts only a few seconds
whereas fascism is eternal
firing squad day & night
can't replace the millions
Time reports shovel squads
digging extra graves for some
100,000 Berliners expected to die
of hunger & cold or commit suicide
Hirohito wipes tears away w/ white gloves
Vice Admiral Onishi's note to ghosts of

his *Kamikaze* corps "souls who fell as
human bullets" Chiang Kai-shek toasts
yellow wine to Mao Tse-tung
humble selves hate enormously
"one heart, one soul, one mind, one goal"
caped FDR at Yalta & death's round vowel
point over his eyebrow how the great man
shrunk into a cigarette holder at first
nobody would believe he died at Warm
Springs it must be a mistake
"take two" yells Joe Rosenthal
in the shuffle ripple U.S. flag on Mt. Suribachi
4-F bad eyes cameraman to
Iwo Jima icon Lt. Harold Shrier
Leo & Paul put together *Monthly Review*
on a kitchen table
will the world be able to recover
now that Taft-Hartley's here
& A. Philip Randolph's been everywhere
while racism slices *The House I Live In*
into frozen Birdseye segregated trays
Cardinal Spellman's red hat round face
wire-rim bifocals pearly pink cherry skin
O Christ your *sheist shmeer* on hot Hiroshima
pavement shadow clutter stained remains
evaporated finger puppet people leap Isadora through
DDT cashmere cloud walls & bop sock hop doo wop
Hucksters concoct unavoidable void
ENIAC cards in steel trays in room after room
menace of Russian communism

Mailer's Naked & 33 year old best-seller suicide
Ross Lockridge Jr. Raintree's brain & Lowry
gin plastered in Mexico when Thomas
Stearns gets Nobel Polaroid in 1948
Baruch before Senate War Investigating
Committee "we're in the midst of a cold war
getting warmer" "I was well liked"
Willy tells Mildred who never knew Ez
38th parallel Inchon MacArthur 62,000
called up for active duty *Dianetics* via
Campell's *Astounding* color TV minimum
wage 75¢ an hour Burn All Reds
kids wear bead chain dogtags
Henry Wallace in Brooklyn speaks
farmer Yiddish to solidarity cheers
weekly rhythm & blues hits
charts top-ten tacked to SAC basement wall
Louis Jordan T-Bone Walker
ah everyone's apart
together
"Burn All Reds
No Mercy For Spies
Rosenberg Traitors Must Die"
anti-prole exploit flicks
"so shocking it was filmed behind
locked studio doors"
home front new wars
orthodoxy of conspicuous
fast car guys camaraderie
terrycloth seat covers mud flaps

Newstand, late '50s. *Photograph by Charles Brittin*

hot rods to hell dragstrip baby
boom everyone's pregnant
military-industrial complex spending
arms production aircraft electronic
AFL CIO merger turns labor into
management's chummy neighbor
on the way up to out
mainland El Barrio mambo
great migration to South Side
culture capital of black America
2200 new arrivals every week
blues clubs crowded slums
storefront churches sluts &
dope gangs blood cops
men fight fires
women in nurse teams
guys rescue gals drive cars
cats & chicks on Geiger crews
streetcleaning/childcare
police/hospital work
air-raid warden/social work
rebuild/emergency feed
Levitt ticky-tacky
white blue pink collared
workers worry about robots
racial mixing
TV's Jim Anderson
benign autocrat
calm cool collected not
garlic armpit Molly Goldberg

not hairball Reilly lunchpail not
life w/ Swedish immigrant mom not
Chayevsky's ghetto pastorals nor E.C.
Menace Vault of Horror Mysterious
Adventures Strange Science not *Mad*
"in the presence of comic books
they behave as if drugged" dear Dr.
Wertham Chuck Berry Johnny B. Goode
Jim Crow "reveal to white masses
Negro qualities which go beyond
the mere ability to laugh & sing & dance
& make music" writes Langston to
gangster nation Montgomery 13
month boycott "there comes a time when
people get tired," tones Martin
"history books will have to pause & say
'there lived a great people — a black people —
who injected new meaning & dignity into
the veins of civilization'" inner city junk
bebop & beyond jones go stone cold dead
sleep deep dreamless *nihil* no-go
Dreiser writes CP/USA "I believe intensely
the common people & first of all the workers
are guardians of their own destiny
& creators of their own future"
frenzy teens dance mindless
system's survivors in white buck Angora
sock hop perfect silhouette combine hoop
crinolines tight belt white sneakers
princess-line dresses black flats

stockings sometimes saddle shoes
what would Ethel or Molly know
when you can't stay or vanish
into gaudy frozen food frieze
or burn away in electric fire
shocked nerves dance
 or vegetalized wives
lobotomy burns away
any real me reality
throw fetus downstairs
die in crash or trash
& draft terrorized guys
agonize on drugstore rubber
hose rites of Trojan warfare
Lenny's desperate Mr. Right
begs the little lady to just touch it
"touch it once" Hubbard's Axiom
"The dynamic principle of existence —
SURVIVE! The reward of survival activity is pleasure"
"The ENIAC computer developed in 1946
first electronic digital computer had
18,000 vacuum tubes & used 140,000 watts"
wait for the screen light to break into bodies
on a diamond or fracture jawbones in the ring
or contemplate test-pattern's fact of being there
to see after midnight when snow or dark prevails
primal survive amazement durable trance
night sky to hearth to pixels
the fix is fact the stare's a given
vanishment isn't banishment instead

immersion in forget forgot for what
"Eisenhower's a dedicated conscious agent of
the Communist conspiracy . . .
largest single body of Communists in America
is our Protestant clergy," writes Welch
to Birchers everywhere & reiterates
Federal taxes a commie plot
whose ultimate grand design
is to reduce all groups & divisions of
American people into a mental state
where they don't have the slightest idea
of whom to believe or what to believe
about anything
Billy James Hargis
Christian Crusader
anti-com Minutemen
off to fight Chinese commies
train in Baja & Robert DePugh
trumps the bivouac w/ machine guns
mortars recoiless rifles
Loyal Order of Mountain Men Rangers
Illinois Security Force kid in helmet
peers through rocket launcher scope
Dan Smoot reports "The Founding Fathers
knew & Jefferson specifically said
a democracy is the most evil kind of government
possible" Clarabell the Clown
in Hell dodge balls of fire Jerry Lee Lewis
hair tendrils catapult w/ benny manic rage
arrogant confident boogie woogie NRA

rock 'n' roll marksman how white sports were
except boxing hopes black would be battered
out of the picture Little Richard squeals & screams
"have you no sense of decency?" asks Welch
while Schine proves doctored photo
Cohn murmurs "threatening to wreck the army"
smears against windscreen smash summer bugs
pulp polka dot pus blots rush to get gone
young at 56 Justice William O. Douglas rules
segregation's unconstitutional Oppenheimer's
security clearance denied "fundamental
defects in his character" advances in color TV
where's the heart part the hope thing the telos
zing on No-Doz zonk speed to night's finale
in another zippy car on conveniently empty
highway back into a city to sleep the day away
25 foot neon chorus girl Hotel Sahara Las Vegas
Mau Maus Miltown Martinis & Viet Nam names
the 50s & 60s Chou En-Lai beflowered by Nehru
at Rangoon Britain departs from Suez Ho Chi Minh
Bien Phu Nasser topples Naguib & the Jabes clan
flee to France where "Juif" means exile & other
nation-states war to hold each border inviolate
violence either silent or loud backroom old sclerotic
erotic fuck feast jam all holes w/ worn-out elite meat
Jackie Gleason Loretta Young Red Skelton Herbert
Philbrick I Led Three Lives fink in Richard Carlson mask
Martha Raye Arthur Godfrey fires Julius LaRosa
"loss of humility" a disability in the new age
Billy Graham in London converts 34,586

electron microscope enlarges specimen 200,00 times
goes deeply into certainty's textures
atoms smashed into minuscule energy beads
throne of thorns crown Walt Disney's four
54 Oscars & it's curtains for O'Neill as Marilyn
weds Joe DiMaggio & June Haver returns
from 7 convent months to marry MacMurray
Shaver Mystery moves from *Amazing* to *Fate*
Bixby's "It's A Good Life" we work out of a
ghostwriting agency on Sunset UFOs in the hills
Orfeo Angelucci met spacemen in Greyhound
bus terminal met Lyra & Orion ah Orphee really
Neptune of the New of "eternal youth eternal spring
eternal day" "Americans feel they are the most
insecure people on earth . . . a compulsive need to
consume . . . no culture . . . no souls . . . much more
than their just share of the world's goods . . ."
"The business of America is business"
Urantia says in 1955, "It's a great blunder to
humanize God except in the concept of the indwelling
Thought Adjuster . . . The adjutant spirits are the sevenfold mind
bestowal of a local universe Mother Spirit . . .
which belongs more appropriately to the story of
your local universe of Nebadon" "Only one
person in all humanity of whom God has one
picture & that is His Own Mother . . . Most of us
are a minus sign . . . but Mary is an equal sign," writes
 TV's first televangelist Fulton Sheen "Before taking
unto Himself a human nature, he consulted with
the Woman to ask her if she would give Him *a man*"

"Once God is dead & man is deified, man
is even more alone & estranged from himself
than ever before . . . *homo hominis deus*,"
Vahanian writes "your earth would have been
 a garden of joy . . . a garden of everlasting desire
to serve . . . but man's lack of understanding
destroyed the harmony of being on Earth . . . he lives
a lost soul," says another master to Adamski
"a demoralized country neither rebuilds nor
recovers . . . social institutions disappear
skills are lost, knowledge recedes & the pull
of a dark age descends on increasingly ignorant
& suspicious people unable to cope /w a hostile environment . . .
created by a nuclear disaster"
Rachel Carson dedicates *Silent Spring* to
Schweitzer, "Man has lost the capacity to
foresee & to forestall . . . he will end by
destroying the earth" "Nature's Law:
Motherhood" " 'How c-could you?'
she gasped. I had only a moment
before talking to a corpse . . . 'It was easy,'
says I, the Jury. "Over 6,000,000 copies sold!"
"No, my friends, brotherhood of all men is not
a Christian concept: it is unchristian & even
anti-christian. Modernist destroyers of the faith
promote false theory . . . Christians
should not compromise their faith," preaches
Billy James Hargis full pink rose
round unattacked buttock "the second most
important law is TERRITORY" Gerald

L. K. Smith states "I'd ask for an investigation
of the most powerful ruthless organization on earth
Jew Zionism" blind eyes mirror blind clouds
blind mouth makes blind sounds surround
one sees everything die

•

I watch hipsters in Birdland move through smoke
move their moves & mudras
code elaborate Masonic gimme five slip me some skin
solid daddy-o what's happening what's shaking

avian display formal trance dancer shadow puppet
hipsters glide in reeefer time to pick up sounds
to dig Bird dig Monk dig Diz Max Bud dig sleek kid Miles

white cats Eager & Woody bankteller bone-ist Bill Harris Albino Red
Rodney noble Dodo Marmarosa Al Haig Tristano dark sparks Cool
Whip Getz

Lester across the street looks down from his hotel window

•

Sunday supplement spirit aka Danny Colt in blue
Lone Ranger eye mask Dick Tracy Crime Stoppers
Notary Sojac the Green Lama Lantern Arrow Hornet
Daredevil's Harlequin suit N.B.I. agent
Plastic Man elastic shape-shifter Eel O'Brien

kinetic film frame frenzy Bebop backed all the way
"Move" at Birdland w/ Navarro Powell Blakey
Curley Russell June 30 1950 mind speed
fractalized solos whose spines petal out
into smoke forests brass tubing blows back
to the bar & against Symphony Sid's WQXR
control booth window a nicotine veneer
smear of villiany smirk as arch-enemy disables
superhero a powerlessness folk opera
geeks cling to in hours of stretched doubt
Bud Powell davening solo "Ornithology"
groan & grunt before Fats & Bird play out
moon theme head & Birdland people clap & laugh
without stunts beyond gravity they fly & crash
into skyscrapers blast through glass doorways
save the day for night & alight in a blur of fur
or feathers or unknown fabric into finale
"I'll Remember April" after Bud's glossolalia
Bird zooms in for fours w/ Blakey
men in supersuits & masks & capes
Kane & Finger's Batman & Robin the Boy Wonder
Wonder Woman #19 Sept-Oct 1946 Help!
1/4 of the world is starving! Will YOU
give that they may live?
"From the mysterious depths of the African jungle
resound the mystic voodoo drums beating
their message of death for the beautiful Amazon princess"

52nd Street Theme can't slow down
time drowns in benny forward flight

64

●

45s of *Bird with Strings*
"East of the Sun" "Just Friends"
the end man the lyric leap over
curlicue viola waves
cellos violins & no-chin big Van Dyke
Mitch Miller oboe noodle between choruses
"Laura" "Easy To Love" "They
Can't Take That Away From Me"
"Dancing in the Dark" *Fantastic
Story Quarterly* & "The Day
The Earth Stood Still" klatu
ooblah doo & racks of paperbacks
torpedo tits push angora limit
Shiva multiplying arms on
Bagavad Gita Signet

●

"blood's still the best most durable cement"
wrote Goebbels in 1931 "we are something
like Christ-socialists . . . Christ
geniuses of love . . . opposite of the Jew who's
hate's incarnation . . . an anti-race . . . poisonous
bacillus" "Hitler understands the absolute
evil of social democracy . . .
where everything's decided by the majority"
Nakano Seigo lectures at Wasada U in '39
"The student body of the University of Freiburg
announces its determination to carry the fight

against Jew-Marxist undermining of Germany
. . . public burning of Jew-Marxist writings
May 10, 1933," rector Heidegger writes
"Knowledge & its possession as National Socialism
does not divide classes but binds & unites people
in the one great will of the State . . . our Fuhrer
Adolf Hitler . . . let's give a threefold 'Heil!'"
"You took the part that once was my heart"
Lady Day sings & kids watch slow pan
along pyramids of bones teeth shoes eyeglasses
instant banish vanish of Hiroshima Nagasaki
"We have completely broken w/ the idolization of a landless powerless
thinking; we see the end of all philosphy which could serve it"
Rector Martin in Leipizig "for truth
is the revelation of whatever makes a people secure"
I can't get started
these foolish things remind me of you
Billie sings & kids see time's end
future's past
we're slingshot shotput out of orbit
nothing'll ever be the same
nothing'll win the game
modern's over & were already post toasties
you & the night & the music

•

ARE YOU BLOND? IF SO
YOU ARE A CULTURE CREATOR
& CULTURE SUPPORTER!

drive Volkswagen
a strength-through-joy car
putter down Autobahn off ramps
into Bop City sidewalk where
schwartzes gavot & cakewalk
brazen singular hip chill decidedly
anti-fascist like Diz & Bird
"The Jews are our destruction"
Reich Minister Dr. Goebbels
gobbles air out of God Bless America
White Power Bird powerhouses through
Cool Blues "Never Open Your Door For
Niggers" "White Women Don't Let Jew Run
T.V. Influence You or Your Daughters:
Whites Associate W/ Whites"
Star Eyes demon Octopus
puppetmaster Hebrew mammon maestro
I didn't know what time it was
Moose the Mooche w/ Candido on congos
sitting-in Woody Woodpecker
movement out & out-of-it doesn't mean nowhere
it's beyond where where's supposed to be
on a map of meaning everything's up for grabs
a shower of enlightenment red & gold rose petals
rains down on downy Aryan body hair sparkle &
pubic baroque yellow white weave
cats attend chicks trick fantasy
meet in heat & tenderness
feed Valhalla a meal of manna
shields in unshattered night

●

Rugby plays *Brief Encounter*
the year Trinity drops its bombs
the year Hitler kills himself
& next year
Xerography & Nurenberg trials

●

"If you haven't fallen by the Royal Roost
you haven't lived" Miltown downs
psyche inside turban opped atop suburban
Groovin' High wigs softasilk two-toned
festive dips for corrugated chips
"Pleasure helps your disposition"
scribes Camel pre-Joe hack plopped
in Saarinen's womb chair lit by
pole lamps watching TV in the family area talk pit
for sponge silence
'48 first fintail Caddie Loewy's '53
Studebaker coupes Wide-Track Pontiac
mobiles like gyroscopes & windbells
tube into your sheath glue sealed lips
w/ Futurama boomerangs & gather
socially on sculptural amoeboid sofas
in a pushbutton instant electrocute
Atomburgers & Birdseye frozen food
at the Royal Roost
the Metropolitan Bopera House

at Broadway & 47th Street
call Sid at Circle 6-2500 for Sid
WMCA "I suppose it was when
the clouds opened up
over the Nagasaki target . . .
pretty as a picture. I made the run
let the bomb go —
my greatest thrill" "It looked
like Ebbets Fields after a doubleheader
with the Giants" *A Night in Tunisia*
Kenny Dorham after Bird
works midrange not supersonic Diz
"pure modern progressive jazz"
— The growing struggle between Two
Great Powers to shape the postwar world
Soviet octopoidal tentacles drape over globe
no time for hysteria
no time for panic
this suit's made of shredded lead
against atomic rays
MacArthur's shades
syzygy energies
Bags into *Scrapple From The Apple*
Dave Lambert & Buddy Stewart
obligatto *Deedle* Bird
fillls before last chorus
then *What's This* they sing
& we sing in a cab to the subway
sing on the BMT back to Brooklyn
"There'll soon be an end to this cold &

wicked war when heardhearted Communists
get what they're looking for"
I'm forever blowing scaddllyabbledoodlywah
bubbles
the rabbi chants the 23rd psalm
yea though I walk to the electric chair
after two more jolts Ethel Rosenberg
met her Maker
she'll have a lot of explaining to do
"I don't mean to say
& no one can say to you
that there are no dangers . . . but
we can hold up our heads & say
America is the greatest force
God has ever allowed to exist on His footstool"
says Ike "The holocaust is nothing but
an invention of Jewish-controlled media"
"Snow White Face Powder
get hip get straight
it's designed for the skin you like
costs a mere 25 cents at your drugstore
call Circle 6-2500"
"What is Bop?
we have a little pamphlet
send a stamped self-addressed envelope
if you'd like to find out"
some 4000 A-bombs stockpiled
6 Sangik Races of Urantia
red orange yellow green blue indigo
"American artists surpass European peers

at MOMA show DeKooning Pollack
Motherwell Gotlieb" Thorazine &
Resperine hit the scene w/ Polio vaccine
racial segregation banned in public schools
fools walk in where angles fear to thread
coonskin berets 1 billion comicbooks sold
per annum ban lurid crime/horror comics
to kids under 18 or year in prison
Dodgers won the series beat the Yankees
1955 no jive & 18 had a draft card
Daily Worker seized by IRS "right
opposite the Strand Theater
the gone styles" subway turnstile
we slip over & under to wolf up what's left
of night two guys scat *All The Things You Are*
 life is stuff beyond what isn't
Jumping With Symphony Sid "this morning
everyone's here at the Royal Roost
Serge Chaloff Conte Condoli Woody Herman
Monte Kay Mildred Bailey & don't forget
at the Royal Roost it's the modern pure
progressive jazz where you can relax"
first H-Bomb popped off last year in
the Marshall Islands & Hemingway
gets the Swedish dynamite but last night
4000 A-Bombs stockpiled while in '55
Bird dies & cats slide into grief oblivion
on a slow boat to China "he's our next
heavyweight champion of the world Ezzard Charles
dig the going sounds & the going people"

•

gone out the door space
life's lived within
gone as far out as too much
gone as all sounds are gone
but those on wire
tape or acetate
voyeur into foyer spook
drop hefty mike down
over heads of heads heading out
air-checks "Dizzy Atmosphere"
at Billy Berg's in L.A.
"Newsreel ready. Incidental music wrong.
Will be re-worked," writes Goebbels
a decade earlier squirrels are hungry rats
w/out bullwhip tails "A Night in Tunisia"
bodies freeze in barbed wire snow
death seized in black & white
"My Old Flame" "Moose The Mooche"
"Lover Man" Jimmy Bruno's piano
1946 global sickness
saturates eternity w/ toxic forever
Prinz-Albrecht-Strasse's *Housegefangnis*
"& there was that terrible thirst"
Charlotte Delbo
in Auschwitz
Law For the Protection of German Blood
boycott Jew business
shops will be photographed

"Off Minor" bang-flash Hiroshima
drive-ins Cinerama 60 mm Cinema-
scope "Un Poco Loco" Bud plays
three different Blue Note takes
muff groan & mute deaths
refuse their lives forget them
they are numbers a cluster of sound
in between takes Wolff & Leica
move through the studio
streaked w/ cigarette smoke
"what strikes you about the way
a Jew talks & sings?" dance
in horned hat & breaking glass
smashed by *judenblick*
pulp evil orb & crack
juden-nase horrid prong
judensau squirts milk to
Jews & piglets in choir stalls
batwing blood-suckers
in cribs for dibs on
Aryan fuel the snow commando
worked eight hours a day
tempo tempo shovel snow
make a path for power's boots
Jerusalem's lost hep! hep!
"The Jews are our destruction
they brought about this war"
writes Goebbels "*Die Juden
sind schuld!*" the Jew's to blame
"Now's The Time" Bird plays

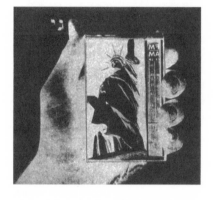

doing the hucklebuck in a web
of nylons wrap the spider egg
output of sub-man of sub-world
crawls down walls into honey
pure condensed blonde milk
shot from breast plate tins
Valkyrie aim canons into spotlit sky
moiling w/ flack & low-flying gargoyles
"Gone With The Wind" Pres plays
down the block from Bebop
near the Famous Door closed by M.P.s
can you see awake German soul
rising sun of Shinto sword rays
veil mazes great wall of paper
soji screens conceal
eyeglasses & beaver teeth
behead Gulliver Yank pilot
wireservice frontpage terror
they stand around headless Terry
laughing
in B-movies masqued by Chinese
Austin App papier maches
Der Furher a man of art & peace
zero Jews killed Faurisson says
Great Migration of jazz heroes
"living doll" Bird at Boston Hi-Hat
runs "Ornithology" to the moon
then "Cool Blues" Twardzik
overlays outside inside the root
bugs Mingus just us & them

face each other groovin' high
young death crematoria so much junk
sarcophagus bedsheets flame
just us just them just is

·

Slim Gaillard overturns Yma Sumac
"Soony Roony (Song of Yxabat)"
laughin in rhythm o voutee *La Libre
Parole* freed world Dreyfus' enormous
nose busy eyebrows phrenologic Juif
map of gross de Gobineau Protocols
Renan inspired by Bakunin Wagner
Das Judentum in der Musik "repellent
eternal aliens" *Le Peril Juif* "Babalu
Orooney" *Der Sturmer* "Jewish children
& teachers expelled from school"
gift gas birds battle w/ song "Jews
carry bacilli of the worst kind
& infect souls everywhere
parasites" Adolf mines his
kopf campsite *"dreckjude"*
"I am the filthiest woman here
I let only Jews call me dear"
Die Judenfrage answered
Endlosung the final solution
"Yo Yo Yo" bongo serra boraxo
rinso *Rassenschande* race defilement
Reichskristallnacht week of broken glass

shul stable horseblanket Torah
"corpses of girls on the river bank
where they used to wander
without seeing their days"
Aigo! Aigo! naked girls cry
"Stupid America!" a field of
watermelons, a dead horse
"Yip Roc Heresy" corpses
a cost accountant tabulates
guards open stalls where they fall
out upon each other in stacks
others heft onto carts
pull them out to pits or pyres
fat kapos "what you got
you make it do" sings Slim

·

"I Mean You" Monk & Bags
1946 "Water! I can't see anything"
beggars tramps Gypsies alchoholics
homosexuals Jehovah's Witnesses
"asocials" whores w/ contagious diseases
the work-shy Reich Central Office for
Combatting Homosexuality & Abortion
killl *negerbastarde negrido* retriever Jung writes
"Aryan consciousness has a higher potential
than the Jewish" *Wird der Jude uber uns Seigen?*
Ein wort fur die Weibnacht "Will the Jew Be
victorious Over Us? A Word for Christmas"

November 18, 1935 Tubingen theology prof
Adolf Schatter prints 50,00 copies "Criss Cross"
Sahib Shibab's alto punches Monk's notes
cubist loop pool Bags arcades black modern
antisemitism antibolshevism racism nomads
create on the move *staatseingehorige*
Herr Bernhard Losener "Race Specialist"
of Interior Ministry *juden schwarze* jazz
Lovecraft's "At The Mountains of Madness"
in *Astounding Science Fiction*
& in '38 Hubbard's lst sci-fi story
"The Dangerous Dimensions"
War of the World on the air & history's
Bendetti's tape & wire segments
Bird's continuous Mosaic arise
towards might's night
to infilitrate & seep through Pasteur's
broken bio seals endless hunger
fury to be "her whole burned body
maggots breed the appearance of
crust of a crab . . . I applied oil
seaweed every means I could think
to save her life" "he died
as he was about to drink water"
beboppers serge margins for clues
structure rapt irrupt Bird blows
in echo maze telephone booth
"(Back Home Again in) Indiana"
DPs parade through DDT clouds
shrouds "look at the piles of bodies

imagine those poor residues of flesh & bones
as your father your child your wife"

•

Trotsky Charlie Chaplin Shylock Abel
Abieser Abimelech Abner Absalom
Ahab Ahasja Ahaser ah Esther the 17th
book whose name was once Hadassah
Boots Szold in Rockville Center
married to Morty pushed her taut tit
into infant mouth & talked analysis
to this kid reading *Ulysses*
Jews in politics in culture in business
Jack The Ripper Jew *Die Rothschilds*
my birth year is Buchenwald's

•

'38 Siegel & Shuster sent *uberjude*
from Krypton to Mutual Network
Biro in Argentina invents ballpoint
Ethel & Julius in *Daily News* flash
her eyes half-closed
small lipstick bow pursed as if in disdain
his spectacled brown eyes look through mesh
new Hiss probe by Nixon in marmot dark
Dagwood 5 o'clock shadow
all German Jews turn in passports
July '38 I.D. cards issued
carried at all times

shown on demand
Israel & Sarah line up for Buchenwald transport
born in my birth year their deaths
Israel & Sarah large red letters painted red *Jude*
Star of David over store windows *Judenaction*
"We have to think of the future & therefore can not
allow ourselves to let in such foreigners
for the sake of immediate advantages;
such advantages would undoubtedly soon become
the worst of disadvantages"
Swiss Federal Council March '38
won't let Israel & Sarah garden roses
grow children fill days w/ *haimish*
delights they pull out raw tripe from slaughter
slurp it down endless gullet for cunning
it's okay "one can recognize the remaining
traces of the red "J" on their passports
in '43 Swiss chemist Albert Hofmann
has the first LSD trip a year later DNA
V1 & V2 rockets fall randomly on Britain
Israel & Sarah have their kidneys cooked in first microwave oven
"the time of the atom bomb was about summer
mother was writing a letter
when there was a flash
roof tiles & glass broke" pencillin

•

1950 General Field Theory
Israel & Sarah in wheat jungle

run through verdant torment to find their lost son
Israel & Sarah tangled in Pollack barbedwire swirls
Izzy & Shu-shu on the floor on a pallet stoned red light
envelopes their pad in blood heat cool
George Pal's *Destination Moon* 10" LP
soundtrack album Chesley Bonstell matte
"A robot may not injure a human being or
through inaction allow a human to come to harm"
one of Asimov's three laws "Klaatu barada
nikto" "Bernie's Tune" piano-less Mulligan's
quartet at The Haig w/ Chet the cherub
hood in dialogue w/ Gerry's swayback certitude
Mel Henke on Wilshire too
Watts Dolphy in his backyard ambix shed
Rodia resurrects cast offs into spires
aspiring cathedrals of broken uprush
Herms in Larkspur dredges up refuse
pigment redeems waste
gnostic garbage assemblage
flawless intangible her wide band
bra strap's hard to unhook after
chugaluging Chilean Reisling
in dark green round bottle
her broad back her harlequin hornrims
wide open precise mouth
our tongues Tom of Finland
Sweet Gwendolyn in peril
handsome Dan in apron
on all fours licks Mistress's
7" stiletto heels patent leather

glare compact Betty Page
in *Titter* Goebbels tells them
"Hitler decides: demonstrations
should be allowed to continue
withdraw the Police
once Jews get the feel of
popular anger, it is only right"
buckled nylon rayon undergarments
canyon cleavage
Exotique: Bizarre & Unusual
"Perry delightfully reached for the
lovely silk stockings & slipped his trim
ankles into their soft goodness
. . . It's *never* too tight
I'm just so excited
that's why I gasp so much
excruciatingly secured laces
reach the pit of his tummy
force him to arch his shoulders
throw out his chest & fairly gasp for breath"
— Fat girl! fat girl! cries Leon Parker
bari chug to Navarro nova
Scope, Pix, See, Glance, Peep Show
Wink, Eyeful, Flirt, Bare, Stare, Rave
Night & Day, Keyhole, Paris Life
autopsy to see w/ one's own eyes
observe watch imagine spy
"I want to get back to the hotel
& see a blood-red glare in the sky
Synagogues burn . . .

information flows in from all over the Reich:
70 synagogues are burning der Fuhrer
orders 20-30,000 Jews arrested" Evelyn
(the Treasure Chest) West
Tempest Storm
Lily (the Girl w/ the Educated Torso) Lamont
Marilyn Monroe Irish McCalla dries herself on mink
Eve Meyer "to the hotel
windowpanes shatter bravo! bravo!
synagogues burn like big old cabins
one fire after another
it is good this way
insurance companies won't pay them a thing"
Rector Martin at Freiburg "*through* the Volk
to the destiny of the state *in* its spiritual mission
are *equally original* aspects of the German essence
. . . the National Socialist revolution
is bringing about the total transformation
of our German existence [*Dasein*]
The Fuhrer alone *is* the present & future
German reality & its law . . .
to the man of unprecedented will, to our Fuhrer
Adolf Hitler — a threefold *Sieg Heil!*"
Yetzirah's 3 Mothers
Berman's 3 veiled
women angels arise above wreckage
time acretes as treasured waste
ancient triune unifiers can't signify
shattered *s'frot* junkyard shards
pious prayers gather like homeless

scavengers dig into garbage for aluminum
cans & bottles by the pound
"Three Little Words" sings Astaire
in a medley w/ Red Skelton in 1950
M.G.M. bio-pic of Kalmar & Ruby
Tin Pan Alley pitchers of song
"since my little sister's right eye was
 put out nobody likes to play w/ her
but she takes it out w/out crying"
Tetsuwan Atomu launched in '52
manga post-bang-flash-modern
comicbooks afterwards beyond words

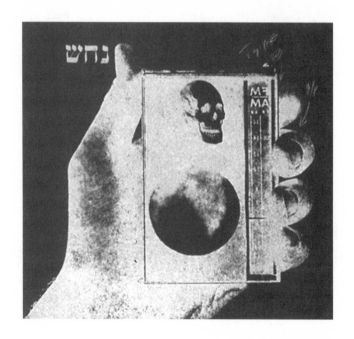

John Altoon & John Reed in Los Angeles, late '50s.
Photograph by Charles Brittin

PRIMO PO-MO

1945 marks Modernity's death & the birth of the Postmodern —
despite whatever theorists, critics, academics, clerks, klutzes, kleagles,
grad students, rad relics, cocktail intelligentsia, faux aborginals, white
midclass mall rats, hip-hoppers, flip-floppers, say or signify. 1945
closes Modernism's file; melts febrile glue of liberal humanism's
Enlightenment's utopic elan & generosity; splatter into Nowheresville
all socially sustaining (& framing) institutions & discourses. 1945 is
the fissure (not Body by Fisher nor Eddie Fisher, "Oh Mein Papa" or
chess' Glenn Gould Bobby Fisher) of Modernity's all-embracing moral
desires; 1945 is the *frisson* of modernism's failure whose seized &
frozen unifying discourses of Popular Front, populism, nativism,
religion, optimism, were, in an instant, erased in nuclear heat
competing with the sun & Fordist *Shoah*. Ideas that once embraced
& comforted become unthinkable before melted shadow-glyphs of
evaporated body stains on Hirsohima and Nagasaki sidewalks.
Discourses & narratives that had reinforced a throng's need for
distinction & separateness were literally atomized. Postwar painters
abandon the human subject, erase & deface all modernist art icons,
turn the canvas into an energy field of pigment molecules, mirroring
the microscopic gaze, in a sense capitulate to reign of science &
technology & anticipating the robotic postmodern & computer-
generated imagos. The Atomic Era received with a similar
dichotomizing frenzy as the Information Age, reinforced by a barrage
of flack & PR promoting freedom,transcendence, glory, & progress
linked with yet another new technology. The postwar wound makes
the unthinkable real & the real inexplicable. More significantly, future
becomes impossible, no longer thinkable. Uncertainty becomes a sure

thing despite TV and its expanding marketplace of positive thinking self-help manuals of how to put Humpty back together again. God dies again as rightwing fundaments boner out of an ever-percolating primordial lagoon, joined by newborn again Yale conservatives, & "new" ullulates end time in print & TV ads w/ added "improved", instability of perfection is an essential huckster given; arose Norman Rockwell Vincent Peale on a heaven-bound escalator; *Peace of Mind* says Rabbi Leibman, *Must We Conform?* asks Robert Lindner, cultural cross-dressing *Black Like Me* by John Howard Griffin ("I had my last visit with the doctor in the morning. The treatment had not worked as rapidly or completely as we had hoped, but I had a dark undercoating of pigment which I could touch up perfectly with stain. We decided I must shave my head, since I had no curl. The dosage was established and the darkness would increase as time passed. From then on, I was on my own."₄)

J. Edgar's anti-commie tracts are master narratives or slave/master narratives that pour forth onto the broken fuel of fear fairytales ("The Fascists and Nazis were not the only menace to our internal security. To their forces must be added the American Communists with their godless, truthless, philosophy of life. They are against the America our forefathers fought and died for; they are against the established freedoms of America. They pose behind a dozen fronts; they have endeavored to infiltrate practically every stratum of life."₅) Damage control, discourse alert, doom, menace, mean boots, pistols, helmets, truncheons, coinroll filled fists, Creature From The Red Lagoon breaks out (in hi-fi stereo) from primal ooze, Communism's ferocious animal hungry for world devouring. Leviathan, whose red and gold scales bear Stalin's janitor broom mustache, drip & drool gore of cannibalized countries & people, floods of blood waterfall darkness expunged into light by row upon row tiers of razorblade shark teeth.

Shock troops of rapacious machinery maws & paws. Clutching
remnants while in the clutches of crustacean pincers, defiled & reviled
by the nation-wide tentacles of The Octopus.

•

queeps & quirps
weetles & blorks
Bill Warren lab sounds
The Man in the White Suit
Guinness boils up immortal thread to weave
indestructible eternal garb
giant ants *Them!* A-Bomb mutants
gobble up deserts & head to L.A.
Johannesburg riots against apartheid
5 years later HST orders up H-Bombs
Martian Chronicles next to
Ray's *Dark Carnival* Arkham House
Orphee shortwave muse
Nat's butterscotch "Mona Lisa" Miltown
1.5 million TV sets next year 15 million
"no one knows better than I myself
I'll go my way by myself alone"
"a beautiful masterpiece of Fashion
Suspense, Adventure, Discipline,
Thrills, in a sinister castle . . .
featuring the exploits of Secret Agent
U-69, her aunt, Fifi the Maid, &
several booted conspirators &
Gwendoline's double . . . featuring

buxom Dolores Du Vaughn
strapping model Suzan Sands
into a new unique leather punishment
harness as part of a sorority initiate
8 poses in chained Chastity Belt & Shackles
2 rope Bondage 2 Wooden Stocks poses
3 arms spreadeagled bondage poses
3 Strait-jacket spanking poses
8 Spanking poses & 18 different
High Heel Lingerie poses
(4 while holding whip in hand)"
Rosenbergs sentenced to death
Catcher in the Rye Minima Moralia
Miracalo en Milano 'S Wonderful
Leadbelly Stella 12 in-dwell
"new suburbanites are pleased w/ the community
that develops " J.D.s w/ D.A.s lurk
in liminal shadow worlds of black
leather & blue jeans mean angles
of cigarette & T-shirt fights tension
Kabuki formalism
drag the strip strip the drag
go man go
howdy rowdy *oustjuden* what cha doin
so far from duh Lower East Side
in dungarees & slick blue/yellow
silk jacket Maccabees S.A.C.
crank up phono to needle *chazzan* Yosef
Rosenblatt ghost *kvells* out 5th floor window
ariseth into air unsymphonic street chaos

static summer heat Roza Eskenazi
"make us coffee & fill up the *argile*"
nextdoor to Salonika *Waiting for Godot*
Ellison's underground *Invisible Man*
listens to Pops & refuses a white world
de Beauvoir's *The Second Sex*
evangel Billy Graham rails on the spot
where Gillette Blue Blades Friday night fights
yield space to Barnum & Bailey Circus deplaced
 in cycle w/ Rodeo marks seasons
McCarthy's hot on labyrinth Red infrastructure
on TV U.S. Army Commies
Marlon bashed longshoreman fights back
at Newport Jazz Festival cool white tin ears pose
for Bert Stern's *Vogue* cinema scan brief peeks at
Monk at work & sheathed O'Day
in widebrim hat sings to morning lethargy
fidgety on wood deck chairs
"Hey There, You With The Stars in Your Eyes"
Salk test-tubes antipolio serum Oppie's dismissed
Milton Rajonksy aka Shorty Rogers w/ Lighthouse
All-Stars through blows tiki pillars
in beach-bum Hermosa
Chesney & Mulligan at The Haig w/ Chico butterfly brushes
Peacock Lane Nino Tempo & April
Stevens Carmen MacCrae across the street
on Hollywood Boulevard
Viva Zapata! A Jazz Mambo Bernhardt trombone
tenors Giuffre & Cooper June's mate Shelly Manne
drums Carlos Vidal congos *Cool & Crazy*

play 10" LPs in Music City Booths & Tina
shoves EPs down her black leotards & serape
while Larry Fagin rings up cash register
Gloria Woods *Hey, Bellboy!* checks out sales
Eden *Nature Boy* Abez wanders down from Griffith Park
to pose for fan snaps & Larry
stashes cool jazz LPs for home consumption
have been through this before: recent jazz divorcee
Judy's pad near Freeway second floor open house
for drifting players & heads *Walkin' Shoes*
"Most of The Haig's customers are there to
listen to the music & those who aren't
don't matter" *Nights At The Turntable*
pass by Koenig's Contemporary en route to Peggy's
"You & The Night & The Music" Pepper's alto
davens over Russo's chart in *West Coast Sound*
Shelly Manne & His Men '53
Marlon's M.G.M. Marc Anthony
Sexual Behavior in the Human Female
lung cancer linked to cigarettes
T-Zone now C-Zone
Harry Hay Mattachine Society
 says Tom "my cock stands up for the kind of guy
who's usually a mechanic or a sailor . . .
after we climax, unfortunately
what else did we have in common?"
Hart & Paolo's plaint
Roy & Edgar avoid rough trade take pain out
elsewhere down phobic tiers of fear-fixed systems
Donald Webster Cory's *The Homosexual in America*

Daughters of Bilitis "education of the variant"
The Ladder & ONE read at Hollywood & Highland
open-air newstand male teen ardor for Rebel
w/out a Cause & Brando's muscle mouth profile
comfort by Village queers at Waldorf Cafeteria
"not one of us but one who understands"
L.A. queer core American Model Guild Mizer
& Quintance *Physique Pictorial* Bilitis
Mattachine covert coded HUAC
PO peek under posing strap basket bulge
Etienne in Chi town all go down
South where tropic cock fronds curve up
along boulevards going to the Pacific
Carole drives all night to SF
in her grape Charms fibreglass 'Vette
reefer sarapes custard pie in Chinatown
coffeshop watch civilians scuttle to jobs
impossible to decode purple hectograph
daily Chinese menu wood gold paint dragons
yawn mouthfulls of teeth & blood red tongues
"a splotch a blotch be careful of the Blob"
help me help me squeals David Heddison
fly in spiderweb

•

"Fine & Dandy" generic soundtrack for
vaudeville nightclub jugglers tapdancers
shpritzers magicians chorines contortionists
"Fine & Dandy" detoxed by boppers reduxed by Art

Metrano 80's TV lone humster
moves hands in magico mudra schlock finger pointings
misdirection pulls rabbits out of hats not there
or "Perdido" exotic dancer whisks funky
Salome veils between her legs
floss her sex light spangles splatter
underpopulated dive ledge edge where
rowdy lint in subcult margins
Lenny & hipster pitband bottom feeders
sin w/out regret
loaded raw cock
burns to let go what comes back
"In Germany, The Jew will not be
able to maintain himself; it's only a matter of time"
says Himmler in '39
erase their names from tombstones
memorials statues civic ledgers
"since someone who admits that
he's been happily married to a Jewess
for 25 years shows he is badly contaminated
by evil Jewish spirit" "Springtime For
Hitler (& Germany)" triumphs despite Max
Bialystock's will to fail "youths armed
w/ poles, hammers & other appropriate weapons
destroy & loot Jew shops" "smashed windows
offend my sense of middle-class order"
recalls Speer "this is one advantage of our time
— in the Reich's highest office we have
the example of a simple modest
alcohol-nicotine-free way of life"

Bird flies over Hefti's *Repetition*
'47 state of art reach back to Whiteman
jungle elevator into Vienna woods
"Jewry's one of the great negative principles of
world history . . . that night side . . . can't be
understood w/out being positioned w/in the
totality of historical process in which
God & Satan, Creation & Destruction
confront each other in an eternal struggle"
send the Jews away
send them to Shanghai Acapulco Madagascar
Angola Abyssinia Haiti the Guianas
(Guyana French Guiana Surinam)
Palestine Sahara Africa
send them to the moon
send them anywhere but here
or there or there or anywhere else
"How High The Moon"
gramophones sewing machines
typewriters thrown out windows
a piano pushed out of second floor window
bedding hangs from trees & bushes
blooms underwear silk stockings wigs
wipe your asses w/ rolls of Torah
Pachuco tattoo in crotch of thumb & forefinger
involuntary blue time-motion number on inmate skin
Lenny's Navy tattoo on pale white shoulder
full-lipped sheik 8x10 Valentino Turham Bey
oy vey fuck you tie me up fix me get me off
Luther's closest collaborator confidant

Philipp Melanchton was one of Them
bury them elsewhere outside German deathyards
Aryan Valhallas even maggots recoil from
Jew *fleish* rats seek as delicacy
"useless life" *gemeinschafttsfremd*
alien to the community "yesterday
two wagons full of Polish ashes were
taken away. Outside my office
robinias are blooming beautifully"
Wie viele Juden passen in einen Volkswagen?
506, sechs aud die Sitze un 500 in die Aschenbecher
How many Jews fit into a VW?
506: 6 in the seats & 500 in the ashtrays
stash joint in *mezuzah*
"the heads of transported victims were
thrown into a basket like turnips
& brought in the elevator to
the third floor for maceration"
Rontgensturmbann X-Ray battalion
How does the Jew enter a resort?
Through the gate
How does he leave?
Through the chimney
"After lunch
I sat upstairs for 3/4 of an hour
soaking up the sun
right under the roof of our 'bone
whitener' . . . to my right & left
Polish bones lay bleaching
occasionally giving off

a slight snapping sound"
"Why do Jews have big noses?
Air is free"
Shecky Greene in a Hong Kong silk suit &
5 o'clock shadow sips *schnapps*
w/ Las Vegas ice-cubes & growls
"only kidding folks"
"what's the difference between
crucifixion & circumcision?
in a crucifixion
one can throw away the whole Jew"
the whole Jew & nothing but the Jew
in dowdy Ethel dresses clunky shoes
matrons whose secrets flatten inside
girdles girth barrel staves rib
grid beneath black rayon
gefilte heat waves *Gesete*
uber die Sterbehilfe fur
Lebensunfahige und
Gemeinschaftsfremde
Law on Euthenasia for the
Incurably Ill & Aliens to
the Community
exotic Quixote watches her mouth
blow his cut dong smack-numb

•

"Cool Blues" Boston's Hi-Hat 1953
Bird's dry incisive tone

the Georgian dies & Kenyatta convicted
Heidegger's new book Julius & Ethel fry
"How Much Is That Doggie In The Window"
Gemeinschafftsfremd
"aliens to community"
they makes us just & righteous
"resentful hair"
marbleized suet lard weave
good life goad Blimp toad
Parker clams so quick shame don't last
he's onto the next extensive scroll
locals try to keep up w/
"every animal mates only w/
a member of the same species:
the titmouse seeks the titmouse
finch the finch
stork the stork
field mouse the field mouse
dormouse the dormouse
wolf the she-wolf"
"one of the great modernists of all times"
"a great gentleman of jazz"
"spongers parasites poisonous mushrooms
rats leeches bacilli TB syphilis"

•

sponges parasites poison mushrooms
rats leeches bacilli TB bacilli
race anthropologists

economists geographers
historians & sociologists
conceptual groundwork
scientific green light for
implementation of
Nazi racial policy
we're left with less & more
than we can remember or forget
Dr. Mengele from Auschwitz
sent eyes of murdered Gypsies
internal organs of murdered children
the sera of others deliberately infected
w/ typhoid back to Kaiser Wilhelm
Institute for Anthropology Heredity
& Eugenics *Juden nicht erwunschtl*
Judenfrei nur fur Arier Jews not
welcome for Aryans only "My
Funny Valentine" Heine wrote
"where one burns books
one ends ups burning people too"
33,771 Russian Jews murdered at
Babi Yar by Einsatzgruppe
2.2 millions Jews deported
from Germany Austria Czechosolovakia
to Minsk or Riga & shot
gassed or beaten to death
w/ axes iron bars & spades
"curiously, absolutely nothing disturbs me
no pity . . . nothing
I shot the heart

the other 3 the head
brain mass burst through air
3 to a skull's too much
almost tears the head off"
transcription acetate surface noise
cracks w/ audience chit-chat
count out "Ornithology" to
pick-up band of locals keep up
but never ahead
left w/ more less than before
more absence
shortwave silence
G. I. Joe taps S.O.S.
while S.S. crowds the door
"heard a concert this afternoon
between 3 & 4 pm
given by the prisoner choir in
beautiful sunshine
choirmaster once conductor of
Warsaw State Opera
80 musicians
roast pork for dinner
baked tench for dinner"
Hoes: "The cremation of about 2,000 people in 5 ovens took
approximately 12 hours. In Auschwitz there were 2 installations
with 4 larger ovens each . . . Once a month valuables were sent to the
Reichsbank in Berlin . . . gold from teeth melted down & likewise
sent once a month to the Sanitation Office of the Waffen S.S. . . . . The
highest number of gassings in one day in Auschwitz was 10,000.

That was the most that could be carried out on one day with the
equipment available."

•

Parker dies in '55 at 35
U.K.'s Ballard debuts in '56
2 stateside postbomb parables
"Invasion of the Body Snatchers" &
"The Incredible Shrinking Man"
I brood over to this very night
Brecht & Kinsey pass as Pollock
curves out of light into the valley below
Elvis blue suedes
tafetta Doris Que sera sera Day
Dead Sea Scroll War of Sons
of Light & Sons of Darkness
where are we that we're here
stain paper w/lines gone dry
& yellow wood pulp powder
"Brain Rays: Russia's Secret Weapon?"
"a woman's primary rightful & appropriate
place is in the family
& the most wonderful task she can perform
is to present her country & people w/ children"
declared Dr Goebbels
"what can U.S. do to strengthen its defenses against
telepathic coercion?"
by '39 10,000 German Jews killed themselves
Die Schwarze Schmach

the Black curse jazz & Jews
defiant *swingjugend*
Hitler Youth packs gangs *meuten*
crews crowds Kittelbach Pirates
Navajos "Hitler's power
may lay us low/& keep us
locked in chains/but
we'll smash the chains one day"
shut-down astrologers soothsayers
whose star script reveal codes threatening national morale
"Take command . . . get the thrill first hand
Drive The New Dodge Custom Royal Lancer"
Porsche's Volkswagen wins postwar drop-in
drop-out derby in flight to return
Disneyland opens on TV in '55
blacks in Montomgery boycott segregated buses
romantic love convict Humbert
on tour w/ Lolita re-elect Ike & Dick
"Lisbon Antigua" poxes jukeboxes
when all else fails go to the wire
go into the kitchen lab & cook up
Birdseye & Swanson chunks of ice
in aluminum G.I. trays for Joe
back from campus try to remember
what isn't dangerous even opening a door
people are everywhere
kids in the bathroom you can't sit
anywhere eat in in shifts shit in bursts
in public housing vertical bunkers
Moses runs highways over neighborhoods

everyone scatters somewhere or wears out
Arthur Godfrey morning cup of joe
Muddy Waters Chess mated & Rosa Parks
staid put *On The Road* scrolls unfurled
 Cat In A Hat stodgy Charlot
A King in New York entranced Kowalski
Lenny's *West Side Story* place for us
Atlas Shrugged
"failures work-shy slovenly criminals"
"seeing this race en mass decaying
decomposing & rotten to the core will
banish any sentimental humanitarianism"
why is the shoah like no other
what do you/we know of it
other than broken grip photographs
movies horrific remote texts
"an ingenous exchange for
baby sitting at Leviittown allows
Jewish & Christian parents to
attend their religious service
shabbes goyim sit on Friday nights
shayne yids return the favor Sunday morning"
what's next?

•

like Bud Pittsburgh Dodo
'58 Moose the Mooche
a Bop chop blockbuster
"Yeh, this is Mike Marmarosa"

"to eliminate the germ of our present
physical & intellectual decline"
"the Jew w/ the help of his Marxian creed
conquers the nations of this world
his crown will become the funeral
wreath of humanity & once again
this planet empty of mankind
will move through the ether
as it did thousands of years ago"
mein Adolf scribes in the joint
as fellow inmate De Sade Pier
sprockets to *Salo* Benito's
industrial power cocks & cogs
sodomy coprophagia mutilation
hustled to death in '72 *Robbin's
Nest* Thorp's *Viper: Confessions of a
Drug Addict* Burroughs Ace *Junky*
"junk's the ideal product . . . ultimate
merchandise. No sales talk necessary"
"Give Sheaffer's New Snorkel® Pen"
"w/ Satanic joy on his face
black haired Jew youth lurks in wait
for unsuspecting girl he defiles w/
his blood thus stealing her from her
people w/ every means he tries to destroy
racial foundations of those he's set out to
subjugate" *A Fine Romance* Midway Lounge
inside of bathtub painted green like South Seas
"I love you body & soul"
Kraft duch Freude Strength Through Joy

no *Billie's Bounce* on *Reichsfunkgesellschaft*
Freude: joy but Freud, *oy*
Hitler's first car in '23
was a Mercedes now wants a people's car
air-cooled as everyone can't afford a garage
"a family car Herr Dr. Porsche at any price
below 1,000 Marks" asks Adolf in '33 in '38
w/ Professor Meserschmidt
lays foundation stone for VW plant
we went through 2 Bugs then onto a Fox
which Adam took over before trading it in for
a Japanese car "The receptivity of the great masses
is very limited, their intelligence is small
but their power of forgetting is enormous"

•

"In propaganda as in love
anything is permissible which succeeds"
says Goebbels *Reichminister fur Volksaufklarung
und Propaganda* "he must be the man w/ the greatest
knowledge of souls . . . must understand secret swings
of the popular soul from one side to another"
"You'll feel SAFER moving in a Sanitized® van"
das zeichen design *Dasein* "sign in
Mystery Guest on *What's My Line*"
sefer the burnt book in urn of body ash
on a shelf faces bookcases my palm
fits the jar's cold rough textured curve
electric life's unrelenting memory

"stay tuned to Mutual! Its famous staff of
newsmen keep you on top of the news
morning noon & night" NoDoz Awakeners
keep me alert during Korea in my room
wait for the Bomb in a state of poetry
open windows & candlelight in a closet
filled with tins of SPAM & soda-crackers
attack of mutant golems branches scrape
siding residue of burnt leaf smoke
cigarettes in a big round tin "AYDS
proved best & safest on 240 overweight
women & men . . . tested four different
reducing methods: bulk wafers
lozenges pills — & AYDS takers lost
twice as many pounds"
"some kind of man" shot full of holes
face down in Venice sump pump pond
"the Artist doesn't create for the artist
he creates for the people
& we will see to it that the people
in future be called to judge his art"
Adolf proclaims "the age of extreme
intellectualism is over . . . the past is
lying in flames . . . the future
will rise from flames w/in our hearts"
says Goebbels *Kulturpolitic* lightning airwaves
Reichsfunkgesellschaft National Broadcasting
Company NBC opens onto Allen's Alley
"as the piano is to the pianist
the transmitter is an instrument you play on

as sovereign masters of public opinion"
Flusterpropaganda whisper prop not
loud burleyque farts & belches w/ crotch
bulge balloon filled with water leaks through
onto elongated flap shoes & checkered pants
whispered heat in ear hole coil whose spiral
nerve ends fire cock tip swell clit root
Wonderful Town "New York New York
it's a hell of a town" "How Much is That Doggie
in the Window?" I believe for every drop of
rain that falls a flower grows around self-frozen
lovers hold onto separate towers
imagine each other epicly in CinemaScope™
garden tendrils obscure beauty
wrap heroic bodies in green sutures nature wins
Death Be Not Proud junior genius saint
submits to brain cancer in duet w/ Anne Frank
Agee dies incomplete at 46
Thomas Mann expires in Pacific Palisades
face East back to West
next year Brecht in East Berlin
confounds love typewriters
Elvis wins the revolution
"You can *feel the difference* at your gum line"
"Luxurious genuine mink
adorns new Pony Tail Pin-Up
coated elastic band" "Johnny
Grass Head — $1 Grows 10 Ft.
First Year — $1" "surer protection
for your most intimate marriage problems

germicidal protection
deodorant protection
Tested by doctors . . .
proved in hospital clinics"
not to offend but fend off recognition
the nose knows B.O.
5 O'Clock Shadow
sandpapers beauty's milk-white skin
Nixon tricks her mouth raw
varicose veins needs this support
Pom-Pom® Cosmetic Cotton Balls
New Way To Sleep Without Fear
Schonheit der Arbeit
Arbeit adelt
Arbeit macht frei
beauty of work
work ennobles
work liberates
"makes accurate copies in 4 seconds
the all-electric all-dry way!"
Thermo-Fax® racked up
over the bowl hurl green death
into sewage puke the last straw
creme de menthe spew
into fool's drool tide pool
treason charges dropped against Ez
off again to Italy
"every animal mates only w/
a member of the same species"
Thorazine Ginger Man

"titmouse seeks titmouse
finch the finch
stork the stork
fieldmouse the fieldmouse
dormouse the dormouse
wolf the she-wolf" Mein
Hitler comps prelude
to Nurenberg Laws
Cha Cha Cha
American Caruso Lanza dies
Lady Day dies
Singapore anorexics
line up at the check out stand
to be beautiful like Auschwitz
Herrenvolk "blond tall
long-skulled w/ narrow faces
pronounced chins narrow noses
w/ high bridges soft fair hair
widely space pale-colored eyes
pinky-white skin" Rodzinki
conducts Shostakovitch's 5th
"Soviet composers
were good" notes Igor "but
couldn't afford the luxury of integrity"
Cultural Congress at the Garden
we read about in P.M. or *The Star*
or *Compass*
commie symps *arbeiter ring* grandkids
L.Y.L. campers Brooklyn's kid cadre crusade
in *shul* balcony look below to

Moishe Oysher sing *Kol Nidre*
high holy days Vito Marcantonio
Sugar Ray inside TV behind glass
radiostore window silently beats the shit out of
Jake Lamotta the sound turned off
reds clubbed & stoned at Peekskill Paul
Robeson concert glass hate shower
easy to group metastasize into
lizard dragon blind loud
crowds protects purity
"Rose (say row-ZAY) . . . Gay
pink light California Rose
your *all-purpose* wine"
"the day of semi-skilled worker's dying
white collar's replacing blue
this the age of the 'team'"
April 1945 BLOODSHED
AND TREASON "Dear Fellow American
Captain of Police called Mrs. (Gerald L. K. Smith) aside
'Get word to your husband immediately
he's in great danger . . . the mob outside is vicious'
a mob was made up of *500 Jews* organized
instructed incited by J. I. Fishbein
editor of the Chicago Jewish SENTINEL"
"En Garde!
It's the Musketeer
strong men tremble in their boots
women know they'll never be
quite safe again . . . when
a musketeer appears

Lentheric" silence indelibly
masked w/ flack
Vance Packard picks up on
"engineering consent" from
Viennese emigre Bernays
a Freud not a Freudian
social scientist spider
entrap target audiences
who shop 'til you drop
born to shop chop chop
shopping's my life Ernst
Dichter (not *schriften*)
doyen of Motivational Research
who rediscovered the prune
that "joyless Puritan"
"Puts Dancing Highlights in Your Hair!"
"God's presence only in pure blood"
"We shall gather together the best blood
just as we breed our Hanover horse
from few remaining pure-blooded
male & female stock" "Leaves
Hair Shimmering Obedient 'Lanolin-Lovely'"
"so shall we see the same type of breeding
over the next generation of pure Nordic Germans"
"Hair so satiny . . . calls irresistibly for
a love-pat! No more wisps or snarls
or stiff ends vibrant glowing tone
Helene Curtis 29¢ 59¢ or $1"

•

Dennis Morgan sings at Hollywood Canteen
"you can always tell a Yank
by the way he drives a tank
to defend a thing called democracy
& save the world from tyranny"
"a people that does not protect
its racial purity will perish!" Streicher
dissolves out of focus
Triumph des Willens
"Again the Hun is at the gate
again he sings his Hymn of Hate"
pens Ira & Yip
 "there's a mad dog in the manger
let's get out of the woods &
deliver the goods
rush rations to Russia
put pressure on Prussia
if that's propaganda
make the most of it!"
Adolf tells the Hitler kids
"we do not want this Reich to get soft
it should be hard & you'll have to
harden yourselves while still young"
Unsere Fahne Flattere fur Uns
Our Banner Waves on Before Us
Golden Gate Quartet "there were
white men black men
a solid All-American team

every creed & color & every belief
from eskimo to Indian chief"
"it is God Himself who
created our Reich! (applause)"
Ich Hatte eine Kameraden
eternal memorial pyre flame
I Once Had A Comarade
"it's a new day
our flag's unfurled
c'mon let's tell the world"
Judy sings at a kids rally
"Chin Up, Cheerio, Carry On
hang to your wits
we'll turn the blitz on Fritz"
Horst Wessel Lied
scene fades to black
Hitler is der Seig
Jew rat crookback
Benjamin's hunchback
double-headed eagle
cleaved to claw swastika
encircle bronze age
ur-root Valhalla
Cabin in the Sky
Rooney & Cohan
Sam it for War Bonds
bundt und blut und
blasted Pathe eyes
& ears of the World
Leni & Gail Russell

line up w/ Reagan &
Murphy Kelly Astaire
Phil Silvers Lena Horne
Betty Hutton Carmen Miranda
Star Spangled Rhythm Four
Jills In A Jeep This Is The Army
Rosie The Riveter "other girls
attend cocktail bars
sip dry martinis & caviars
making history working for victory"
WAVES & WACS
Up In Arms Joan Leslie
hard sells Ronnie "You don't know
what war's about . . . we're
a free people fighting to be free
free to marry
free to raise a family"
John Payne Lyn Bari
"last night I had a lot of trouble
w/ a woman taxi driver
she wanted me to sit in the back seat"
snaps Bob Hope
by 1940 half of Germany's philosophers
are members of the Nazi party
Aryans arrive fully formed from
heaven in eternal ice dethaw & stalk
earth armed w/ electrical powers
printing press rolls Newspaper for
Blond People *blut und boden*
bloody soil *flusterpropaganda*

shadow speech iron
bomb shard *entartete kunstler*
d.g. artists pus-pregnant rodents
waddle down anchor ropes
dive snout first into one-pot stew
Eintopf das Opferellen des Reiches
pubic quotation marks stuck to tongue
Jung "the Jewish problem is a regular complex
a festering wound . . . it is typically Jewish
that Jews can utterly forget that they are Jews
despite the fact they know they are Jews"
Robert Alda's headaches in Hollywood
Rhapsody in Blue melting-pot *schmaltz*
Fagin props Smith's Folkways box
against Jones Street door
we dig through 78s in Fillmore
Salvation vaults King Records
Delmore Brothers Decca Carters
Roy Milton *Butcher Pete* Parts 1 & 2
Electricity Jimmy Murphy 12 string
Scotty Stoneman's lost fury fiddler dime-store LP
Bluebird brothers Monroe
Columbia Robert Johnson
King Solomon Hill
Vee Jay Mavis & Family spine root
electric branching *New Freedom Bell*
45 Country Gentlemen Blind Willie
Johnson *Country Blues*
Charters network mythography
Mississippi John Hurt & Denson

brings Bukka White back alive
in Coffee Gallery last month Elmer
Snowden in the doorway J.C. Burris
Sonny's cousin Eric Anderson bathe
blues aura reception vessels
of entranced transmission
Screaming Jay Hawkins
demonic sad *I Put A Spell On You*
Jim & Jesse *The Sea of Love*
Red Sovine
Jenks "Tex" Carman *My Dog My Everything*
guys at the club enrapt'd in deep trap of Hank
past Europe's skeletons Japanese fire kimonos
Rusty & Doug drink up the bayous
10 years later benny exact hipster magus
Smith brings it back home over
horror tightrope look down below
Great Depression image industry
camouflaged as metal-framed furniture
flying-saucer lamps butterfly chair
freeform coffee table amoeboid sofa
"You must be born again" chants
Reverend J.M. Gates in a history
without 1933-1945 at each end
city folkniks sharecrop
Appalachian immigrants
ardent Jewish college kids
stoic high country *kvel*
postwar *volkisch* return
trad jazz comeback

"You better get ready for your judgement"
growls Sister Mary Nelson
in Jones Street pad panoramic view
"all these folks pretend us
& all of them hypocrites too"

•

Stalin says "the German racial theory brought Hitler & his friends to
the conclusion that Germans were the only fully valuable nation &
therefore must rule over other nations. The English racial theory
brings Mr. Churchill & his friends to the conclusion that nations
speaking the English language are the only valuable nations & should
therefore rule over the remaining nations of the world"

ice skaters in lower Rockefeller Plaza
cocktails at the Rainbow Room
work out at Reilly's Gym
catch up w/ the U.N. at Berlitz
Giselle McKenzie in Studio B
get your passport but never have to leave
watch Garroway through RCA Exhibition Hall
windows Coty's $100 thimble perfume
enter Dunhill's plutocrat humidor
Taylorite Rockettes high kick piston
engine runs Super Chief out of Penn
westward out of words rocking by
day & night returning G.I.s
sing & cry & give away
lucky coins silver dollars Indian head pennies

to kids in short pants w/ their *shiksa* moms
caught up in flight to & from home
Krazy Kat full moon over stucco
soaks-up pueblo white radium
through ancient window holes
Howard Johnson's rest stop flapjacks choke
maple syrup overcomes four melting butter pats
float over circled rims stainless forks jab
kind nostalgia heartburn of ample extremes

Remove Ugly Hair Forever In Just Seconds!
From Lips . . . from Chin . . . From
ANY PART OF YOUR BODY!
Removed Gently . . . Swiftly . . . Permanently
NEVER TO GROW BACK! Only
$9.95 Complete 2 Weeks Free Trail

skin removed from dead camp numbers dried
bookbinding wallets lanyards keychains belts
suspenders watchbands

skull inkwells candlestick holders
Romantic desk ornament icon mourn
young death of Novalis & Goethe's
sagacious old age snuff ground bone meal
melt gold-fillings into swastika ornament
seeks cleavage heat her saliva keeps you lubed
push it in her *fraulein* gobbler Georg
Grosz in New York City handcuffed

muselmann walk into electric barbedwire
mamzerim scrape tear pull him off
at dawn after roll call
jew bolsheviks ruin the pure possible while
bolshevik jews pass A-Bomb scrawl to KGB
B-movie trickster guys in Brooklyn
smoke Sobranies the Europe embrace
defaces Joe Shmo zombie
yes master whad'ya know
the only way out of here
is through the chimney

•

Heshy, the landlady's son, back from war gave me a metal box filled w/
tiny Nazi propaganda booklets: Hitler touches peach pink cheek of
tyke offered up by an adoring mother to his touring car; amidst blonde
braid cowled Rhine maidens who wait for hours to offer bouquets to
Der Fuhrer; flower festooned radiant Leica bliss saturated rich black
& white worship w/ oldstyle German type on one side of the page
Kraft duch Freude, strength through joy, pinch their cheeks.
Coins medals *Kreigsmarine* sailor ribbons. The Luger he kept & later
blew his brains out in childhood's room, his *yiddishe* mama mopped
& scrubbed blood for two days w/ Bon Ami & ammonia

•

"We live in a time of perpetual peril & the end isn't in sight. I won't
attempt to guess whether this is a thirty year war or a hundred-year
war . . . two struggles — the power struggle & the ideological struggle

. . . Lenin said 'the road to Paris lies through Peiping & Delhi' . . . &
the Moscow-Peiping axis will not yield the road to Western ideas &
allegiance w/out an epic struggle for Asia . . . we'll have to avoid the
sins of self-righteousness & self-delusion. Our power is not absolute
nor is our judgment infallible . . . The tempered use of our power, the
sympathetic understanding of people's 'yearning to breathe free' . . .
constitute the true resources of America & the treasured hope of our
civilization" spoke Adlai egghead Stevenson
of Libertyville, Illinois in '53
"you know why he was never elected? he was too smart" "he was a
divorcee" "his shoes had holes in them, his socks rolled down"

•

"I wouldn't be trapped in the kind of life Mom had —
babies, working on the farm . . .
I was beautiful, talented
I was going to be somebody"
"GENE TIERNEY'S ORDEAL"
"You can't live down a bad reputation"
"Liz & Eddie's Hideaway Ranch!
The Plot to Get Sinatra!
Startling Report!
Diary of a Bachelor in Europe!"
"We traded our baby for a tractor"
"Dear God:
As I start down the long road to womanhood
guide my footsteps in the pathway of righteousness
& protect from all evil that awaits along the wayside"
"104 POLAR-TRAPPED

KISS-STARVED G.I.s
picked the army's champ woman-chaser to
take *their* furlough by proxy with
two gorgeous dames! 287 Certified LAUGHS!"
"Party Girl — NOW I'M PAYING!"
"Turn A Glance
Into Romance
. . . Have Caressible Curls w/
SPOOLIE Hair Curlers"
"He's Got The Whole World In His Hands"

●

3 years later Berlin blockade & airlift
how many inmates dance on the tip of
a gas cannister
SS sages ponder numbers
percentages Talmudic
defining exacting
where to go
who to stay
who works
who dies
"even the brood in the cradle
must be killed like a swollen toad
we're living in an iron time
& have to sweep w/ iron brooms"
blutkitl blood cement bond
"Jewish textbooks teach
every Jew has the right to kill a non-Jew

it's pleasing to the Jewish God to kill
as many non-Jews as possible"
Life Time Reader's Digest
Saturday Review Atlantic Monthly
Harper's Christian Century
Commentary Commonweal
Hiroshima praise debate
Hersey's book on 6 survivors
Shikata go-nai "it can't be helped"
"a woman w/ a whole breast sheared off
a man's face raw from burn
I can't see anything"
"after finishing the ditches
10 victims strip
are given corrugated-paper shirts
reaching halfway down the thighs
. . . ditch bottoms lined w/ straw
order 10 at a time to lie in ditches
alternately head to foot
Globocnik's men throw hand grenades
heads arms & legs fill the air
. . . shoot anyone still moving
spread lime over remains
new layer of straw
new victims watch
wait their turn
women kicked in stomach & breasts
children smashed against rocks
75,000 killed" "1 A-Bomb =
1 city; 1 H-Bomb = 1,000

Hiroshima bombs" "we're all
survivors of Hiroshima" writes Lifton
whose *hibakusha* talked
from depths of Pandora's box
& D.P. Frankenstein *Death In Life*
crystalline form of hydrogen cyanide
breath & air turn to gas *Degesch*
(German Corporation for Vermin Control)
pesticide kills people pests
Zyklon B I.G. Farben spinoff
prussic acid/hydrogen cyanide
Borman Himmler give out the news
that mystics astrologers & nature healers
manipulated Hess
Eintopf das Opferellen
des Reiches one-pot meal
sacrifice for Reich community
"the fate of the white race is
indissolubly linked w/ that of
their cattle . . . they can't survive
w/out dairy products" says Herbert
Hoover in 1926
homeless stalk streets
drop pants in Clarion Alley
shit & die as thrift-shop scouts
walk by
loss a background music
"ten at a time" into pits
cover w/ lime
s'frot fixed to *Etz Hayim*

blasted apart to fill branches of
Etz Met
zombie *muselmann*
walk into electrified barbedwire
DP pushes shoppingcart against the light
wants it over everyone watches
everyone has other things to do
everyone turns away
everyone knows
everyone allows it

•

book is fact
book survives
book lies
book lives
in their death
book is barrier
book opens the gate
book remembers language
book forgets
book never sets the record straight
book knots the tangles
book hides w/ metaphors
death is the others
writer survives
to right death
but gets it wrong

what's the song
Celan un-sung
Todesfugue
conceal in literature
what was revealed
what can't be faced
erased or replaced
Adorno's no-no
to lyrik poetry hubris
now all love songs
strangle in barbedwire
books about books
theory about surviving as books
theory of difficulty
theory of memory
exclusion & inclusion
remember forget
whose language to tell it in
what language works
that silence hasn't tried
Encyclopedia of the Holocaust
4 volumes Hilberg's 3
volumes Freidlander's 2
volumes fill silent void
w/ silent words
silence between each number
each memory
every second
lost in being found

everyone screams
dreams & forgets
in book's fact
its stillness
one enters
entrapped
unable to leave

•

"once on Leszno Street
a little pauper snatched a bunch of violets
from my hands & ate it"

•

kennkarten
proof of identity
ausweis ID card
S.S. number
unknown but known
set aside or dissolved
into paperdoll protocol

rachitis rickets
unable to stand or walk
kids hide weeks on end &
4 & 5 year olds
forget how to talk

•

Befehl ist Befehl
Orders are Orders
Trans-Lux Newsreels
in Grand Central
uptown & downtown
watch the War
between trains
bringing people back
taking them away
Spam packed IRT rushhour
snoods & fedoras
The Daily News or N.Y.
Times All the News
V-for-Victory
V-Mail
V-Discs
March Of Time
fashion ration
inter-slashed w/
hatch opens
dump bombs down below
instant death gardens
kleiglit cross swords
illumine Grauman's Chinese
Academy Awards
Oskar Werner unable to flee
Germany defiant Jack Palance
doesn't like blond Nazi captive

Attack doesn't like faux albino
studio head Rod Steiger
Johnny Ringo Terry Malloy
Jim Stark in the drive-in desert
Great Wall of CinemaScope
shrunk to pinhole TV news
storytelling *This I Believe*
"I See No Doom Down an Alley"
writes Herbert Hoover
Glenn Ford daddy-o Rick Dadier
disarms J.D. Vic Morrow kewpie
doll Bill Haley's Comets toll
"Rock Around The Clock"

•

bodies piled up like merchandise
impromptu self sings out
Buchenwaldlied
Ach Buchenwald kann dich nicht vergessen
Weil du men Schicksal bist
Oh Buchenwald
I can't forget you
You are my destiny
we eat garbage
while lice eat us
"young boy
tears through a pile of corpses
what are you doing
I'm looking for my father"

"we were supposed to be the chosen people
I never believed that"
gornisht
er iz a gornisht
chosen nothing
chosen for *Leichenkommando*
corpse detail
chosen there was no choice
chosen for nothing
chosen to vanish

chose to close the door
the book
"a human hand
five of us divided
to eat . . . cut out a piece
we were eating"
chosen to eat ourselves alive
chosen to eat our dead
chosen ones & twos & threes
to the left
chosen to be unlucky
chosen to be chance
chosen ones twos threes
chosen for *churbn*
chosen names stories in *churban* literature
live or die turned into books
beyond sight's grasp
chosen to burn bridges
burn history
destroy Temple of mask

whose midnight reveals
an unchosen face & fate
"we were eating
it doesn't matter what it is
as long as there was
something
this was the last place
where they kept us to die
& die & die
chosen to die
no rules
just killing that's all
just killing
chosen for killing
bullet in back of skull
sewing uniforms for killers
"*Moyshe, ikh leb*
bagrub mikh nisht lebedkerheyt
Moyshe
I'm alive
don't bury me
while I'm alive"
chosen to breathe death
chosen to exhale lime
chosen to suffocate
blood shit burst bladders
chosen for another *Aktion*
chosen to educate our children
guide our children & be
nice parents & make parties

& everything but that was all
make believe

•

nursery school *uberkinder* sing
Der Sturmer Streicher "Holy Scripture
a horrible criminal romance
filled with murder incest fraud indecency
& Talmud's the great Jew book of crimes
Jews practice everyday" "fresh dried
powdered blood of slaughtered victims
used by young Jewish couples pregnant Jewesses
for circumcision"
"deceit usury falsehood
aren't sins in the eyes of Jews
who have a different conscience
a different God than we have"
Sign at Employee Gate Ford
Motor Company Dearborn Michigan
1939 "Jews Teach Communism
Teach Atheism
Destory Christianity
Control the Press
Produce Filthy Movies
Control Money"
"we are trailed & hunted
there's no place to hide
our money's gone . . .
we swallow suicide pills"

"gassing sets my mind to rest"
"send them where?"
"Jews represent an extraordinary
malignant glutton"
"the hour will come when
the most evil universal enemy of all time
will be finished
at least for a thousand years"
in Italy Ez sez "Sassoons baboons
Rothschilds migrate to the U.S.
& stink up the whole country . . .
Greek philosophy jettisoned
Justinian, jettisoned
the sense of LAW that built up Europe
puked into discard
don't start a pogrom
that is
not an old style killing of small Jews"
"jews can no longer own bicycles or
typewriters" "Jew rabbit experiments"
"boiled soap out of bones of women & men
which took several days . . . from 3 to 7"
"20.952 kilograms of gold wedding rings"
"they will never believe . . . Hitler set up a
slaughterhouse & massacred 7 million Jews"
in Katzenelson's diary "our war's
primarily a race war" says Himmler
"first & foremost a war against the Jew who
incited other nation-states like England & America
to enter the war against us . . . it is, secondly

a war against Russia . . . the war against Jewry
& the Asiatics is a war between two races"
Auschwittz Belzec Bergen-Belsen Birkenau
Buchenwald Chelmo Dachau Flossenburg Gross-Rosen Maydanek
Mauthausen Natzweiler Neuengamme
Nordhausen Ravensbruck Sachsenhausen Sobibor
Struthof Terezin Treblinka abcedary
phonemic rows of silence
mouth nor page can hold nor let go
unable to explain anything
neither here nor there
between the lines
nobody knows what you mean
"most students remember Hitler as the man who
built the Autobahns & licked unemployment"

•

knotty-pine paneled family room
bubble lamps Saarinen's tulip chairs
womb chairs Con-Tact paper Applikay
picture window indoor-outdoor 3-D TV
'59's 11 1/2-inch 3 1/4-3-4 3/4 doll bod Barbie
teen nosecone tits "if Jews were alone
in this world they'd stifle in filth & offal
they'd exterminate each other
in absolute absence of self-sacrifice
& turn battle into comedy"
"it can't be ignored
we have in our midst

several hundred thousand
former Communist Party members"
I.F. Stone in the *Compass*
"men who make the hydrogen bomb will be fashioning a more
monstrous weapon than the world has ever had before w/ which
to kill people. To kill is wrong. The word for it is murder. The
scientists who create the bomb will be guilty of murder"
Cloud Chamber Music by Harry Partch
Brando in brown face asks new bride Jean
Peters "teach me to read" to end
shot full of twitching holes
Zapata! screams taut Weisman
"next to home & family
the American loves his car most"

                                                 •

"At last in a world torn by the hatreds & wars of men appears
a *woman* to whom the problems & feats of men are mere child's
play . . . w/ a hundred times the agility & strength of our best male
athletes & strongest wrestlers, she appears as though from
nowhere . . . as lovely as Aphrodite — as wise as Athena —
w/ the speed of Mercury & the strength of Hercules —
she is known only as WONDER WOMAN, but who she is,
or whence she came, nobody knows!"
Joe Palooka Skeezix Dick Tracy enlisted
Tillie the Toiler became a WAC
Fritzie Ritz took a war job
Winnie Winkle married a G.I.
Sheena Queen of the Jungle

Mary Marvel long-lost twin of the Captain
Miss Fury & Wonder Woman from Paradise
Island "enlightened land of women"
Swing Shift Maisie Ann Southern
heiress Lucille Ball elects to work
in a defense plant snood & slacks
"I'll be seeing you in all the old
familiar places" sentimental journey
plattered through time as code
for all unsaid detail WW 2
a late night TV movie exotic orchid
watch Fred & Ginger at midnight matinee
warm-up for Lord Buckley
tan "bourgeois divas" Lena Horne
Hazel Scott Katherine Dunham
"they didn't make me into a maid
I became a butterfly pinned to a column
singing away in Movieland"
54 soap operas Young Widder Brown
Mary Noble Backstage Wife
Ma Perkins's son killed in WW2
windows w/ single star flag relics
grief loss widows beyond reason
or devotion Stella Dallas
Front-Page Farrell Romance of
Helen Trent Portia Faces Life
unresolved deaths of G.I. teenagers
silk & nylons vanish go bare legged
or use leg makeup paint a seam line
lacquer dark red lipstick Sweater Girl

Hughes designed brassiere for Jane
Russell's Outlaw bosom
Marilyn in defense-plant job
desiring *Yank* Rita image on B-29
Grable imago on tanks tractoring
over kraut helmets arms & legs
we're all broke up
"the first species of evil
is that which befalls man
. . . the nature of coming-to-be
& passing-away
I mean to say
because of his being endowed w/ matter"

•

"You are a '*sale boche*'
in the name of 12,000 persecuted Jews
here's the document!"
at German Embassy in Paris
Ernst von Rath
mortally wounded by
Herschel Grynszpan
pulled the trigger 5 times
on November 7th 1938
where I wander through numbers
unable to read the map
rot stacks in the pathway of
black men sent to open Dacchau
"outbreak of popular outrage"

Jewish women raped & if he chooses
a German may also torture her to death
"for protection of German blood & honor"
smudge face *maidlach*
what's poetry for
who does it sing against
implicit w/ illicit absence
crushed photograph
time scrape scratch
all particularity erased
a vanished face

•

"Is your office still keeping pace?
Is all work attended to in due time?
CONTINENTAL SILENTA
a noiseless which obviates nervous strain
allows quick undistrubed typing
Wanderer-Werke" "Only one
class are real outsiders to hierarchy:
those who believe the arrangement
according to different laws
laws of reason or social justice
. . . Germany rearranged its forces
in revolutionary process while
Britain reached Dunkerque
on well-worn tracks of Tradition"
"The world in the throes of
economic suicide/The gold illusion:

exchanges of world bread wheat &
foodstuffs are objects of speculation for
private gamblers sanctioned by liberal economy
stage booms & slumps as it suits them
& are responsible to no one"
Gerda Kurz in chorusline of
Berlin's Metropole Theatre
Signal prop solo dancer at Comedians
Cabaret picture essay at Wilhelmplatz 8/9

"During the course of the years, the Ministry of Propaganda has
become a gigantic institute in the form of political control extending
to all spheres of public life &, fortunately for the person concerned,
also of private life."

"The up-to-dateness of this house also finds expression in the fact
that it gets rid of everything antiquated & employs every refinement
of the technical aids the 20th century can offer us. Files of papers are
not so important in this house as the telephone, the tele-writer & the
radio. For speed is the first commandment in a Ministry whose task
it is to care for & guide the nation along its political, mental, &
spiritual path. Its most important instruments in doing so are the
press & the radio."

the Good Doctor's anteroom operator at her console w/ 100 important
connexions which can be obtained directly
every minute of the day & night
politic's world beats its heart
in telegraphic pulse

dit-dit dot-dot

displaced to be replaced
schlep down cobble antique streets
spire shadows gobble Hebe stream
into chalice of malice cauldron
ambix bones & sinew you knew
knew you now know nothing
I sing to myself then out loud
like lunatic castaways in doorways
where plump boojy pigeons boogie
through one offering after another
zapped by ribbon floss zippered through
networks of digital tragedy
credit debit ID cards
know it or knew it
blew it apart in sunspot heat
melt & evaporate water
tree's roots unfold for

•

Andersen the cabaret singer
recorded it for gramophone
Lili Marleen by Hamburg poet Hans Leip
music by Norbert Schultze PENKING
Portable Cooking Plants/Washing
Machines/Kitchen Ranges
a demonstration of German efficiency
"The Japanese state visit to Berlin:

Matsuoka greeted by Goring &
The Fuhrer . . . ROOSEVELT —
Emperor of the World!" by 1940
FDR owns West Indies Canada Central
South America Alaska Siberia South East Asia
Australia South Seas Greenland Iceland
North Scotland Ireland Azores &tc
Snapshots of everyday ZEISS LENS
the eagle eye of your camera at Jena
where philosophes JU88 Junkers
Flugzeug Dorndorf Shoes Zoot
Suiters Jitterbug 2 new American
slang terms explained by SIGNAL
"In L.A. adolescents w/out
regular employment form gangs
murder & burglary clubs make L.A. streets
unsafe at night . . . seamen stabbed in the back
on empty streets like the swingboys
young Mexicans wear strange trousers
wide at the knees & narrow at the ankles
three-quarter length coats & hats like those
worn in Europe by poets & composers . . .
the hall resounds w/ unbroken streams of jazz
& swing boys & girls dancing w/out
high spirits & gaiety but the latest climax in
indecency & degeneracy . . . not unusual or
chance eccentricities but a widespread symptom
affecting ever-widening circles . . .
psychiatrists publish diagnoses of it . . .
unstable foundation of American society

undermined . . the colossus reaches further
. . . internally insidious poisons . . ."
Molotoff in Berlin . . . Tanks break through
the Stalin line . . ."

•

WHAT DOES A SOLDIER DO ON LEAVE?

1 :   a ration card for 14 days leave receives
cards for 10 lbs of bread & cake 2 lbs of meat
1 lb of butter 1 lb of provisions macaroni etc
1/2 lb jam 1/2 lb legumes 1 lb of sugar
1/2 lb of coffee mixture 1/3 lb of pure coffee
2 oz of tea 1/4 lb of chocolate
2 eggs & 4 pieces of cheese
soap shaving soap & soap powder

2 :   his mother

3 :   his friend

4 :   his fiancee

then everything will be done by itself

•

"shadow of a man
sitting on the steps

at the time of the blast"
there not here
everywhere else
gone somewhere
or nowhere
where do you imagine
or invent a place
he vanished from
erased to
what was his face
after it saw
what it first heard
what word or sound
in unleashed light
turned to see
if anyone else saw

•

Heli Deinboek singt Randy Newman
Bruder Bruno
1996 tomorrow
Berlin chooses
Holocaust Memorial
12 million bucks
meanwhile
back at the Bank
Swiss hitters
dole some of it
out in Alzheimer

absent mindlessness
Claudia's blond cheeks burn
Christian's pink crewcut bristles
forgotten trashcompact chains
dark star cipher history confounds
implodes Freieuniversitat American
Studies as Bronx Jew agit-props crude
them/us und Maxine mit David
bury their dreidels & stash
chickensoup ladels deep freeze
dis-ease the palpable target
feels as death's *Anisakis simplex*
spirals into your guts but
we're not the ones
they're not the ones
okay who are they
where are they
who aren't there to declare
where they were &
who you were in their
violent rage & blind fury

•

Khruschev
Supreme Council of Soviets
on 20th Century Fox soundstage
Can-Can in production
Sinatra's elevator shoes
MacLaine's underwear

"Man's face is more beautiful
than his backside"
Man's Fate Modern Library
 "What do you have to sell us?"
Jealous capitalists compete to eat
each other alive
boycott Soviet crabmeat
"Urbane yet light-bodied
Hathaway's Batiste Oxford '56"
eyepatched class pirate baron
Tsarist diplomat scion like Nazis
wear the coolest clothes in *Life*
Wilson's *The Outsider* turtleneck
caterpillars inside sleepingbag on
park lawn facing British Museum
next year Jack's Kerouac hits the road
to martyrdom stardom the pause
TV inhales eternity smoke ring
fast cut before station break

•

Hiss jailed a month before Bar
Mitzvah mitzvah & Fuchs
at Old Bailey too late
Soviets have the Bomb too
saw first run of *Call Me*
Madam Merman Mesta
Sobell off to Mexico
Hollywood Ten in slammer

Hammett dries out
it's way past *Ko Ko*
Bird's got 5 more years
Jack The Dripper's here
J. Fred Muggs is there
wax lit Liberace at Dumont
Crazy People turn into Goons
absurd's the word
demoted to commonplace
former lurid clarity
fission shatter unity
"a thousand suns"
elided dictionary
no more yes
Miltie's seltzer showers
bowers of mutants
w/in & w/out
yisgadal v'yiskadash
Who knows One
cut off my hair
I've read my portion
done devotion
you were my witness
we share the world to come
my *derashah* remains secret
enter community
received by unity
in between *bris* & death
a liminal teen
in Levi's a Levite

bebopper & puffer of
Mamala's pilfered Chesterfields
Zippo stoked
we awoke in L.A.
May's warm flanks & muff
against my butt
barukh adore
out the door
into dawn's early light
shadow over shut door
her mother snored behind

•

What's This bops Dave Lambert
Buddy Stewart oh everybody's here
at the Royal Roost saw Serge Chaloff
for only 90 cents everybody's here
saw Woody Herman he's standing at the bar
saw Charlie Ventura Conte Condoli
how about that
everything's original at the Royal Roost
the Metropolitan Bopra House
you can sit back & relax & hear
the gentlemen in the flesh
from 9:30 to 4 o'clock in the morning
& kill yourself saw Aleister Crowley
swap sigils w/ Harry Smith & Arturo
dragged Vladimir inside a manic curve
Marcel & Peggy sip sanguine

gin & tonics to *Anthropology*
Margaret Mead's saddle shoes tap on beat
Mailer & Jimmy Jones work hard to
get w/ it "the great Charlie Parker &
the All-Stars" digging the gone styles
Edward Everett Horton divest ducats to
covert hipsters Pops & me sit ringside
flashbulb Speed Graphic glove fits our duet
in black & white blaze of suave disdain
backstage Leonard Feather politics for
race/gender parity & John Hammond
dispatches frontline telegrams to *Down Beat*
& *Masses* & *Mainstream*
between 47th & 48th street across the street from uh
Snake Pit

blame it on Virgil Aaron & Marc
WPA pop-front thirds & fifths
narrate rivers & lost lands
to radio word from Manhattan ateliers
world ghost voice through aether
sways to Lenny blur calligraphy
Robert Shaw's the monitor
"Will you be the one?"
Icarus marionette montage
unfold flipbook descent from Empire
State tower Kong hugged
turrets & scalloped chrome
"Leningrad Malta London
Rotterdam Manila Warsaw

Guernica" "Before he leapt
we saw a guy" cry out
spine shrapnel cut in two
spool around
 chakra crack-up
ballad of hurry-up "clear
the props" "take off
your thick electric glove"
comicbooks in foxhole
united front of fixed faces
voices all of it Hollywood
19 year old farmhand
guy from Brooklyn
Jew Italian noble Negro
first to die in totempolemics

Groovin' High School Confidential
vs Hot Rod Gang rumble on the docks
love on the rocks
bobbysox untamed youth
rock around the clock
dance shocked bodies
shell shock hipster trance
offbeat slo-mo snap
of cool fingertips *Don't
Blame Me* "It's Like a Kinsey
Report on the Campus" dot-dashes
Winchell for *College Confidential*
cops club Bud down defending Monk
"the greatest piano player in the world"

Much Macho Machito Afro
Cuban Salveros *Manteca* mambo
voyeurs at Palladium slide into star
sequins & black silk si si
her body/mind split I yam
thought/I'm mind's muscle
Rene's bifurcated heart
chewed into strips
junkies tie up w/
down for the dip
trips death zipper
opens up & gives up
gut tongues tasting air

•

how about a great big hand for a wonderful guy
a wonderful group
Charlie Parker
blow dad go
Ornithology
over the moon
below the belt
V-2 rocket fuel
blasts off mozzarella
gleam sticky strands
cat's cradle
tattooed lips
ah you're a livin' doll

•

Cadence obits Carson Smith
bass on Mulligan quartet dates
Carson City Stage
bodies pile up in history hamper
new kid in L.A. looks into Ray Avery's window
at just-released Pacific Jazz 10 inchers on display
hey it's an old guy routine
see who dies today
to say I'm alive
eggdrop soup spooks
reconfigure yesterday
unplug bowl bliss ripple
spiral down slimy tubes
am here they're gone &
me w/ them & them in me
in segments splinters partial
allure of precise romantic
Claxton & Willoughby photos
in Wilshire Haig underage
w/ half-sister Joan in
bomb tip bra clamped inside black
angora suave chic hip come-on

not just death but all the time it takes
to accept death's companionship
its *gemeinschaft* whispers in your ear
mists its waxy furls w/ desire
Bruckner & Mahler

Dean & Hopps have my lost
manuscripts & George & Diane
have letters in folders somewhere
we're bound together in liminal
forward march w/ crooked side-steps
sand-dance shuffle out of focus
out of the picture into photographs
people remember when
you were alive w/ them
when you were part of their lives
when we all were together
going somewhere everywhere

•

Kerouac's postcard
"Don't call me Mister
call me Jack"

•

Palladium Ballroom l954 mambo
drive-in movie Moab Utah *High Noon*
"Rock N Roll
Sputniks
Flying Saucers
Now
Edsel at Levelland Texas"
in 1949 USSR explodes its first A-Bomb
"We have no time left" Truman's Oval

Office looks into a rose garden
"The final decision of where and when
to use the atomic bomb was up to me.
Let there be no mistake about it."
"This is the greatest thing in history.
It's time for us to get home"
H-Bomb a thousand times more power
than A-Bomb, streetcar ran over
Teller's right foot in Munich
wears a leather foot to pester the AEC
Military Congress cluster to build it
"It's either we make it
or wait until the Russians
drop one on us without warning"
"In some crude sense
which no vulgarity
no humor
no overstatement can extinguish
physicists have known sin
& this knowledge they cannot lose"
countered Oppie
but sin wins at Livermore
at Eniwetok atoll in Marshall Islands
fall 52 ion chambers
high-speed cameras
beta-ray spectrographs
uranium & heavy hydrogen
core heat 5 times greater than the sun
"in the end there beckons more & more
general annihilation," Einstein says of

Frankenstein shadows blanket Korea
Soviets explode their H-Bomb in Siberia
in 53 & second US test at Bikini atoll
drops death sparkle confetti
on boatload of Japanese fishermen
"When the air becomes uranious
We will all go simultaneous"
Dean skids out in 55
more major than future's erase
dislocates grief from old soldiers
never die they just fade away
tones mom's makeover Mac
Arthur custom cut leather jacket
aviator shades Emperor of Japan
angry Avalon combats shame by
deferring to pain's mirror

I'm you & there's Suzy Parker
"thank God for high cheekbones
the truth is so dull & I come from
a Ku Klux Klan family" Revlon's new
Futurama case w/ lipstick refill
"unearned suffering is redemptive"
Martin Luther King tells his flock
"it's nice to be in people's fantasies but
you also like to be accepted for your own sake"
says Marilyn chewing on a rhinestone earring
"they'll wear toilet seats around their necks
if you give 'em what they want see"
3-D glasses red blue *House of Wax*
Vincent Price & Charles Igor Bronson paddle ball

SCTV ball wah-wah containable terror
not unimaginable chain reactions
totem coonskin Crockett caps for kids
zombified by Disneyland whitebread
stuff phonebooths & VWs (Hitler
bugs) crewcuts bond *bund* in cram
ram hula hoop multitude back onto
TV dancefloor Dick Clark chaperone
plantation master benign MC droodle
prototype Happy Face Texas Chainsaw
leatherface lurch after those nurses
chlorophyll clean fresh mouth
kill anything palpitating
in Yakima 1947 "nine saucerlike things"
1200 mph hold a candle over Bridey Ruth
Simmons Murphy hypnotist Morey Bernstein
regress to 19h century Cork while others
met the future w/ bomb shelters linked
like pop-it beads across the States terror
sheathed in nuclear tube dress or pink
side stripe rogue trousers real George
& yo-yo's a nose-bleed blow-lunch
hardee harhar nerd dork snakebite
war against the regulated Squares
"We love everything: Billy Graham
the Big Ten Rock & Roll Zen applepie
Ike — we dig it all," announces Ti-Jack
"we're the vanguard of a new religion"
"I'm nearsighted & psychopathic anyway
America I'm putting my queer shoulder

to the wheel," writes Allen & Rexroth
"I write poetry to seduce women &
overthrow the capitalist system" "Sincerity
is the quality that comes through on TV,"
said Nixon l955
"McCarthyism is Americanism
w/ its sleeves rolled" said Joe
"Communism is Americanism"
proclaimed C.P/U.S.A. Foster
"I'm glad we're on television . . .
millions of people can see how low
an alleged man can sink," said Joe
"I continued singing
I suspect I always will," said Seeger
"You want to shut up every Negro
who has the courage to stand up & fight
for the rights of his people &
the rights of workers," said Robeson
"I'll be glad to do anything to help
anything you consider necessary or valuable'
said Gadge "I'm sorry I have no way of
remembering that," said Odets
"Come On-a My House" "Tutti-fruitti
all rootie!" "Sh-boom!" vodka
production heats up in Cold War
"bad stuff drives out the good since
it's more easily understood" writes
Dwight Macdonald & Mickey Spillane
in T-shirt looks like McVeigh
way to go "I didn't know

it could be like this" Grace
Metalious Peyton placement
Flair Mad TV Guide Jet Playboy
Milton DeLugg & Jerry Lester
mug like moths around stoic Dagmar
"Are you self-employed?
Do you deal in services?"
What's My Line third-degree
Gorgeous George & Antonio Rocca
Friday Night Fights from the Garden
saloon jocks jab & jolt Sugar Ray

•

how easily narrative falls into place, realizes itself through a
story-telling historian who sets out to frame a tangled constantly
permutating chaos into a familiar & repeatable story w/out shadows
or dead-ends; how impulsively memory organizes into a choir to tell
a story of what it remembers symphonically, i.e., formally; even
experimentalists practice w/in or against forms that have formed
their relationship to writing & telling stories;
history is the story of writing

"my late wife Tina & I in the days, us kids in profile digging jazz
or who knows?"
Photograph by C.R. Snyder

NOTES

1   "The Power of Self Destruction" by Paul Tillich in *God & the H-Bomb*, edited by Donald Keys. New York: Bernard Geiss Associates, 1961. Page 24.

2   *How to Survive an Atomic Bomb* by Richard Gerstell. New York: Bantam Books, 1950. Pages 138-139.

3   "The life of the addict is a living death." From a booklet by a Christian publishing house with a massive hypodermic needle on the cover.

4   John Howard Griffin, *Black Like Me*, Boston: Houghton Mifflin Company, 1960, Page 14.

5   J. Edgar Hoover, Address at Annual Commencement Exercise, Holy Cross College, Worcester, Massachusetts, June 23, 1944, in *J. Edgar Hoover on Communism*, New York: Random House, 1969. Pages 63-64.

SPECIAL THANKS

The author & publisher would like to thank C.R. Snyder for the use of his photographs & Kristine McKenna for her help with the photographs of Charles Britten & the artworks of Wallace Berman.

The various artworks are by Wallace Berman. On pages 107, 111, 123, 143, & 151 are collages from his publication *Semina*. On pages 73 & 83 are verifax collages which were used in Jack Hirschman's book *Black Alephs* (London: Trigram Press, 1969). The collage on page 47 is from the cover of *Third Rail* #9, 1988 and the one on page 127 is from his estate. Thank you Shirley & Tosh Berman.

Tip of the hat to Robert Briggs for publicity efforts & early enthusiasm.

COLOPHON

Set in *ITC Berkeley Old Style* a type face based on Frederic W. Goudy's original design for the University of California in 1938 & released by Lanston Monotype in 1956 as *Californian*. Tony Stan redrew it in 1983 for the digital world of typography. As with other Goudy faces, joyous idiosyncracies enliven in an oldstyle new style of way.

Titling is *H-Man*.

book design by J. Bryan

DAVID MELTZER began his literary career during the Beat heyday in San Francisco, reading poetry to jazz accompaniment at the famous Jazz Cellar. He is the author of many volumes of poetry, including *The Clown* (Semina, 1960), *The Process* (Oyez, 1965), *Yesod* (Trigram, 1969), *Arrows: Selected Poetry, 1957-1992* (Black Sparrow Press, 1994), and *No Eyes: Lester Young* (Black Sparrow, 2000). He has also published fiction, including *The Agency Trilogy* (Brandon House, 1968; reprinted by Richard Kasak, 1994), *Orf* (Brandon House, 1969; reprinted by Masquerade Books, 1995), *Under* (Rhinoceros Books, 1997), and book-length essays, including *Two-Way Mirror: A Poetry Notebook* (Oyez, 1977). He has edited numerous anthologies and collections of interviews, including *The Secret Garden: An Anthology in the Kabbalah* (Continuum Press, 1976; reprinted, Station Hill Press, 1998), *Birth: Anthology of Ancients Texts, Songs, Prayers, and Stories* (North Point Press, 1981), *Death: Anthology of Texts, Songs, Charms, Prayers, and Tales* (North Point Press, 1984), *Reading Jazz* (Mercury House, 1996), *Writing Jazz* (Mercury House, 1999), and *San Francisco Beat: Talking With the Poets* (City Lights, 2001). His musical recordings include *Serpent Power* (Vanguard Records, 1968; reissued on CD in 1996) and *Poet Song* (Vanguard Records, 1969). He teaches in the Humanities and graduate Poetics programs at the New College of California. He lives in the Bay Area.